The Occupation

The Occupation

War Memoir of a Boy

Kelly S. Medina

Library of Congress Control Number: 2009907640
ISBN: Hardcover   978-1-4415-5918-0
               Softcover   978-1-4415-5917-3

This book was printed in the United States of America.

To order additional copies of this book, contact:
Xlibris Corporation
1-888-795-4274
www.Xlibris.com
Orders@Xlibris.com
55618

CONTENTS

PREFACE

While this book is about the experience and life of the author during the Japanese occupation in the Philippines until the termination of the Second World War in the Philippines, it begins with the simple life of Filipino people before the arrival of the Spaniards in the early 1500s and the Spanish regime that concluded after the arrival of the Americans and, thereafter, the Japanese occupation. The story is related by a boy who has a firsthand experience of the war and his observation of the ruthless treatment of Japanese soldiers toward the Filipino civilian, which started right after they set foot on Philippine soil. This book also includes an interview of old acquaintances who shared their own war experiences.

I am greatly indebted to the authors and publishers of the sources from which the material for this work was taken and to those who made themselves available for my interviews and otherwise assisted me in completing this book. I am particularly grateful to Mr. James Helt and Mrs. Sandra Helt for helping me in editing this book. The photographs used in this book are from the National Archives, Washington, D.C., and also from the *By Sword and Fire* by Alfonso J. Aluit, *The Guerrilla Resistance Movement in the Philippines*; *Cabanatuan* by Dahk Knox, *Flyboys* by James Bradley, and *The Rising Sun* by John Toland. I owe special thanks to several Japanese friends who provided me their war stories they themselves experienced, which enabled me to find merit in this book.

Kelly S. Medina
27 April 2006

INTRODUCTION

The Early Philippines

The written history of the Philippines begins with the arrival of the Spanish conquistador. Before this time, the Filipinos were part of a big empire, and the Rajah governed the country. The religion was Islam. It had its own trading system with other countries and commercial trading with the Arabs, Chinese, and probably Japanese. They had their own spoken and written language and dialects. The early inhabitants were from Indonesia and Malaya.

In my travel to Indonesia, I found that their language is very similar to a combination of Tagalog, Ilocano, and Visaya. Of course, their present language is mixed with Dutch, in the same way that the Filipinos have a mixed language of Spanish, English, Chinese, and little Japanese. There are Indonesian root words similar to Tagalog: *tutup* (to cover or close), *bulan* (moon), *matahari* (sun), *bugas* (rice), *tubii* (water), *ama* (father), *ina* (mother), *anak* (children), etc. The mountain people of Mindoro, known as Mangyan, have their own written language.

When the Spanish conquistador under the leadership of Ferdinand Magellan landed on Philippine soil on March 17, 1521, he was sent by the King of Spain to look for spices, but he did not find any spices, but did find death in the hands of a native chieftain of Mactan named Lapulapu. That was the first Filipino encounter with the foreign invader. The Spaniards pulled back to the sea, continued their search of spices under Sebastian del Cano, and returned to Spain and reported their findings and discovery. The

King instead sent more conquistadors via Mexico; one of them was Loyaza expedition in 1525 and followed by Villalobos in 1535. It was Villalobos who gave the name Las Filipinas in honor of Prince Philip of Asturias, who later ruled Spain as Philip II. King Philip wrote to the friars of the Order of St. Augustine in San Augustin in Mexico City.

> We have been informed that while still a layman, you went with the fleet of Loyaza to the Spices Islands and you remained there for eight years in our service. As we now charged Don Luis de Velasco, our Viceroy in that New Spain, with two ships for the discovery of the Western isles toward the Moloccas . . . We commission you to go with the ships and to do whatever might be ordered by the said Viceroy.

Upon receiving the Royal Order, Fray Urdaneta drew up three alternative routes for the expedition organized by Don Luis de Velasco. One proposed route was to proceed to the Philippines, another to Guinea, and the third to Japan. But he was opposed to the route for the Philippines. He wrote to King Philip.

> There could be some scruple or impropriety in making that voyage that your Majesty has ordered to be made . . . For it is clear that the Philippine archipelago not only falls clearly within the terms of the pledge [the Treaty of Zaragosa] but the point which projects toward the East is in the meridian of the Moloccas Islands, and provision of this agreement are, in effect, that none of the fleets of Your Majesty or of your vessels can enter, or settle o trade . . .

The Viceroy died, and the King gave the charge to Don Miguel de Legaspi as Captain-General of the expedition, who set sail immediately, and entrusted him with a sealed letter that carried his instructions, including his final destinations. It was not to be opened until he was three hundred leagues away from the Mexican shore. On November 21, 1564, the fleet sailed from port of Navidad. Knowing that they had reached the three hundred leagues, Legaspi assembled his officers aboard his flagship and opened the sealed letter from the King. It said their final destination was the Philippines. On their landing on Samar Island, Legaspi proclaimed sovereignty of the entire archipelago in the name of King Philip. At the island of Leyte, the Spaniards were well received by Rajah Malitik. Legaspi sent a peace message to Rajah

Sikatuna who was convinced of the Spaniard's sincerity. The peace treaty was ratified by the blood compact wherein both men drank from a cup of wine into which their blood had mixed. When the Spaniards went to Cebu where Magellan was slain, Rajah Tupas, thinking that the Spaniards came back to avenge their losses, met them at the shore in battle array. After a few skirmish, Rajah Tupas surrendered and acknowledged himself a vassal of the King of Spain. Thus, began the conquest of the Philippine archipelago.

They started recruiting Filipino natives and armed them to fight against their own people. In early 1570, Juan de Salcedo sailed in company of 30 Spaniards and 500 Filipinos and attacked Mindoro, the home base of pirates. Accompanied by Martin de Goiti with 120 Spanish soldiers and 600 native allies, he sailed northward to explore the island of Luzon. They found a very large Muslim settlement situated in the opposite bank of the Pasig River in Maynila and Tondo. Maynila was defended with clay mound around its perimeter and bronze cannon on top of the mound. Rajah Sulayman, also called Rajah Mura or young Rajah, commanded the fort. Goiti attempted to make peace but was denied. He laid siege on the palisaded fort and razed the settlement to the ground. Rajah Sulayman withdrew to the other side of Pasig and regrouped his forces, readying for another struggle. After looting the abandoned village, Goiti returned to his ship and sailed back toward the south. Salcedo missed the action; he was exploring the Taal Lake. Later he joined the Legaspi expedition. After Goiti informed Legaspi of his findings in the north of a big harbor and a big settlement, they made plans to return to Maynila with a force of 210 Spaniards and 1,000 native allies and sailed north. In Maynila, the Muslim chieftains were not ready for the war and were not ready to succumb but were quickly overpowered by the better-armed invading forces. On June 24, 1571, the formal and solemn celebration of the foundation of the city of Manila was held.

The Chinese began infiltrating the country; they settled on the south bank area of the Pasig River known as Parian. The Spaniards, being aware of the expanding population of the Chinese, decided to establish a Chinese colony where the Celestials had their homes and shops where they worked with iron, brass, and silver; bought and sold wares; and served as carpenters, bakers, and tailors to the city. The Chinese believed that Manila was rich in silver so they sent a fleet of Chinese junks. After learning that there was no solid mountain of silver, they returned to China. The arrival of the Chinese mandarins disturbed the Spanish authority, and they prepared to defend the city. A Chinese leader named Eng-Kang, known by his Christian name Juan Bautista de Vera, ordered every Chinese to give him a needle so that he might know the number of people available for the uprising. The number of needles reached to 22,150; he knew that he had enough strong men to fight. He planned to attack on November 30, 1603, St. Andrew's Day.

However, before the Chinese could attack, a Filipina woman went to Fr. Juan de Talevera and betrayed their plot, and he immediately relayed the information to the authorities. Both the Filipinos and Spaniards were warned in time. Eng-Kang was arrested, sentenced, and put to death. Again on the night of Friday, October 3, 1603, the Chinese unfurled their dragon flags and attacked Tondo and Quiapo, setting the buildings on fire and slaughtering the population. The Filipinos and Japanese were repulsed by the attackers. The Chinese retreated to the mountains of San Pablo, Laguna, and made their last stand on October 20, 1603, against the government forces of 200 Spaniards, 300 Japanese, and 1,500 Filipinos under the command of Don Cristobal de Axqueta Menchaca.

CHAPTER 1

The Freedom Fighters

On June 26, 1892, Rizal arrived in Manila; masonry was growing rapidly. Rizal had brought with him a copy of the Constitution and By-laws of the Liga Filipinas, a society that he intended to establish and that he hoped would unify the Filipinos and eventually lead to their emancipation from the Spanish rule. At the time, Rizal drafted the rules of the Liga in Hong Kong. He knew that masonry was succeeding well in bonding the Filipinos, but he was also aware that the fraternity has its own limitations. Under the ancient landmarks of the Orders of Masons, members were prohibited from using the fraternity as a political organization to overthrow or bring down a legitimate government. A young man named Andres Bonifacio had come up with the idea of forming a new and different organization to supplement the work of masonry, and this was the birth of the Katipunan. The initiation was very similar to the Masonic rituals. Rituals taken from Carbonari, Illuminati, Sublimes Maitres Parfaits or Sublime Perfect Masons, Raggi, Lega Nera, Centri, and Guelfi. Secret passwords and secret recognition signs were also used. In July 3 of the same year, the Manila lodges arranged several banquets in his honor.

Rizal enjoyed only a few days of freedom.

On July 7, the local papers published his arrest and deportation to Mindanao. The entire fraternity was shocked and bewildered. Six masons who were present at the founding of the Liga met in Binondo and agreed that it was time to establish a new and more radical order, one with separatist aims. They called this radical movement Katipunan.

The masons responsible for the creation of the Katipunan were Deodato Arellano of Luzon Lodge; Jose Dizon, the Master of Triangulo Taliba; Valentin Diaz; Teodoro Plata; Andres Bonifacio; and Ladislao Diwa. The Katipunan was based on a constitution and by-laws similar to the Liga with some changes or innovation to suit their needs. An example to this was they devised three degrees for the Katipunan just like a symbolic masonry, but instead of calling them *Aprendiz Mason*, *Companero Mason*, and *Maestro Mason*, they named them *Katipon*, *Kawal*, and *Bayani*. In masonry, the members wore aprons while in Katipunan, they wore hoods over their heads. A brother guided them through the ceremonies; they called him *Mabalasik* (Terrible). The most important innovation in the ritual was the introduction of the so-called *Pacto de Sangre* where neophytes were required to incise their arms and sign their names in their own blood. This was not a Masonic practice, but a ritual copied from the Carbonari. Though there were differences with the Masonic ritual, because of its similarities, many Masons who joined the Katipunan were confused in the cross-examination. When Emilio Aguinaldo was initiated into the Katipunan by Andres Bonifacio, he kept responding to questions in "the Masonic manner," said Santiago Alvarez. In subsequent years, the resultant structural similarities between the Liga, Katipunan, and Masonry, and the subsequent discovery that all these organizations were led by the same group of people, would justify the conviction of the authorities that they were in fact essentially united and made the government feel perfectly justified in considering Masons ipso facto subversives.

In one of his essays, Rizal had described eloquently what universal discontent could lead to.

> All the little insurrections that have hitherto occurred in the Philippines have been the work of a few fanatics or mutinous officers who have had to deceive or cajole or exploit their followers to achieve their ends. Therefore, they failed; all of them. Not one of these insurrections had the people behind it; not one sprang from a whole race's need; not one fought for the rights of man or the claims of justice. This being so, they left no lasting impression on the memory of the people. On the contrary, once the people's wounds had healed and it recognized itself to have

been the victim of deceit, it applauded the fall of those who had perturbed its peaceful existence. However, suppose a movement were to arise from the people itself, with the miseries of the people as its motive power? What then?

The revival of Liga occurred when Andres Bonifacio, Apolinario Mabini, Domingo Franco, and other Masons took advantage of the relaxed atmosphere and reactivated the Liga under the governance of the Supreme Council that had several councils under it. The most active, popular council was in Trozo headed by Bonifacio. There was a split between several popular council; one of which still nurtured the conviction that political reforms could be wrestled from Spain through peaceful means and the other, led by Bonifacio, which argued that the time for revolutionary radicalism had come. This caused the dissolution of the Liga Lodge.

Filipinos uprising against Spain

Persecution of Masons

In March 1894, the persecution of Masons resumed with greater severity. The Masonic met in hiding. The friars were using the Civil Guards in searching, arresting, and destroying Masonic groups. The Masons therefore adopted an ingenious scheme to masquerade their meetings. While a meeting was taking place, a purely social affair was usually held in another room to divert the attention and lull suspicion.

A year later, a reign of terror for Philippine Masonry began. The abuses of the authorities spread throughout the archipelago. Arrest and deportation of members became a daily occurrence. However, the losses of Masonry gave a spectacular growth in the Katipunan. For example, a certain Lodge Taliba was "dormant" because its Worshipful Master and Bonifacio were heavily engaged with the affairs of the Katipunan.

CHAPTER 2

Spanish-american War
In The Philippines

In 1897, a conflict between United States and Spain was in progress. The American sentiments toward the Cuban struggle against Spain was at high gear, just waiting for a reason to start a war, and it happened when an American Battleship, USS *Maine*, was blown up and sunk in Cuba. The Americans found an excuse and blamed Spain for the sinking of USS *Maine*. This ignited the Spanish-American War. At the same time, the Filipinos were staging their own revolts against the Spaniards in many provinces in Luzon and Visayas. President Theodore Roosevelt sent a message to Admiral Dewey, the Commander of the Asiatic Squadron in Hong Kong, directing him to proceed to Manila Bay and destroy and sink the Spanish fleet. Emilio Aguinaldo was waiting for an opportunity to return to Manila to continue the struggle. To avoid appearing in court, Aguinaldo, accompanied by two of his trusted aides, left for Saigon where he took another boat for Singapore, arriving there on April 23, 1898. Upon his arrival, he was contacted by the American consul in Singapore, E. Spenser Pratt, who talked to him about joining forces with the Americans against the Spaniards. Aguinaldo was persuaded. Emilio Aguinaldo, hearing about the Spanish-American War, contacted Admiral Dewey who agreed to join forces to attack Manila. At that time, all provinces were under the Filipino Army; the only Spanish territory left were the Cavite Naval

Base and Intramuros, Manila. Aguinaldo was in Hong Kong with several revolutionary members. Aguinaldo had received four hundred thousand pesos from the Spaniards (for unknown reason). The revolutionary exiles wanted a share of that money, but Aguinaldo used the money to buy arms and ammunition for the revolutionary army. He took the arms to the Philippines and distributed it to the revolutionaries.

In April 23, 1898, the American consul in Manila had been ordered by the home office to evacuate; and shortly before noon on April 25, Dewey received the cable from the Secretary of the Navy with the instruction: "War has commenced between the United States and Spain. Proceed at once to the Philippines. Commence operations particularly against Spanish fleet. And you must capture vessels or destroy. Use with utmost endeavor." The Spanish fleet in Manila was commanded by Admiral Patricio Montoyo, a distinguished naval officer. The Spaniards had more ships, but they were lighter and had fewer guns. The American fleet had more tonnage, was better armed, and the men were better trained and organized.

On April 30, 1898, Admiral Montoya maneuvered his fleet into battle formation. Dewey meanwhile was on his way to the China Sea. At five o'clock in the morning of May 1, 1898, he was in the outer limit of Manila Bay anchorage. The Spanish gun emplacement in Fort Santiago, upon seeing the American fleet, started to fire, but the range was too far for the cannon balls to reach. Dewey picked up his telescope and sighted the Spanish fleet in crescent formation off Cavite, and the battle had a beginning.

Following Dewey's victory over the Spanish fleet, the Filipino revolutionary junta in Hong Kong urged Aguinaldo to return to the Philippines and lead the revolution against Spain anew, taking advantage of the arrival of the Americans. On May 19, 1898, Aguinaldo had a joint conference with Dewey, and they mapped out their operations. One by one, the barrios fell in the hands of the rebels. Soon, vast areas of the Tagalog region, Bicol, and Ilocos were freed from Spanish control. The Spaniards tried to rally the Filipinos to join forces against the United States, but it was too little and too late, and all efforts failed. The sea was controlled by Dewey's fleet while the land was controlled by Aguinaldo's Filipino army. The Filipino army occupied the area around Manila. The Spaniards were offered an opportunity to surrender, but the Governor-General Basilio Augustin declined the offer. Aguinaldo shut off the water supply and waited for hunger and thirst to complete the job. While this was going on, the Americans were arriving, the first under General Thomas Anderson, the second group under General Francis Greene, and the third group, which arrived on July

31, under General Arthur MacArthur. Dewey arranged with the help of Belgian consul, Edward André, to negotiate with the Spaniards for the surrender of the city. The Governor, finding out that his position and the city could not be defended, made an agreement. When Spain learned about the surrender terms, he was relieved of his post by General Fermin Jaudenes. However, Jaudenes also found that the city was no longer tenable. To save face, he entered into a bizarre compact with the Americans whereby a mock battle would be staged and after which the Spaniards would surrender on the condition that the Filipinos would not be a part of the said surrender. And Dewey agreed.

The American fleet started bombarding the city, and General MacArthur's troops advanced to the walls. General Aguinaldo, who saw all this happening, refused to just stand by and do nothing, so he deployed his men close to Intramuros. Later the Spaniards raised the white flag of surrender. The mock battle was over, and Manila had fallen.

Aguinaldo went back to Hong Kong and issued a decree, setting up a dictatorial form of government. Aguinaldo decided to declare independence of the Philippines. In the afternoon of June 12, 1898, in the town of Kawit, Cavite, the independence ceremonies were held. The Philippine national flag was unfurled. Aguinaldo asked Marcela Marino Agoncillo to make the flag in Hong Kong. In August 1898, five Americans and five Spanish commissioners met in Paris to discuss the peace terms between Spain and the United States. On December 10, the Treaty of Paris was signed; it provided that Spain would cede the Philippines to the United States for the sum of twenty million dollars.

On October 21, 1898, President William McKinley issued the Benevolent Assimilation Proclamation in which he declared that the United States would assume control over the entire archipelago. He instructed the military commanders to extend American conquest over the archipelago by force. In the early hours of the evening of February 4, 1899, an American patrol advanced toward San Juan, east of Manila, which was off limits to them to ascertain the presence of Filipino troops in the area. Suddenly, four men loomed before the patrol. "Halt," the American Private Willie Grayson yelled. One of the men ahead moved. "Halt," Grayson yelled again. "Alto," the man yelled back, and Grayson fired. The man on the other end dropped. Grayson had fired the first shot in the Filipino-American War. Because of this, the Filipino-American War erupted, which lasted for three long years. There was heavy fighting between the Americans and the Filipinos. There were many casualties.

Between February and March, more American reinforcement arrived. They launched offensive in the north and south of Luzon; by the end of March, they were at the gate of Malolos, Bulacan, the capital or the seat of the Filipino Republic government. Aguinaldo moved his government to San Isidro, Nueva Ecija. One of the Filipinos' great tacticians, General Antonio Luna, who was educated in military colleges in Europe, was the Chief of Staff of the Filipino Army. He was one of the best to lead the Filipino army to fight against the Americans. While he was making preparation for the defense of Pangasinan, he received a telegram to see Aguinaldo in Cabanatuan. Unfortunately, Aguinaldo was not present, and instead, General Luna was met by Felipe Buencamino, the secretary of foreign affairs, with whom he had a bad confrontation in the past and on whom he now vented his irritation. At the stair, a group of soldiers fell upon him with guns and knives, and he was killed. Filipinos, learning about his death, were severely demoralized, which caused Aguinaldo to retreat to Palanan, Isabela. The Americans, realizing that Aguinaldo was slippery than an eel, planned to trick him. Assisted by some Filipino allies posing as Filipino army escorts with Americans posing as captured soldiers, they were able to gain access to Aguinaldo's camp. They were received as captured American soldiers, and while the Filipinos were celebrating, the Americans showed their true identity and overpowered the Filipinos in Aguinaldo's camp. Aguinaldo was captured and returned to the city of Manila where he took an oath of allegiance to the United States of America. After which, he issued a proclamation appealing to the Filipinos to accept American sovereignty.

CHAPTER 3

Philippine-American War
The American Occupation
In The Philippines
1898-1902

The Filipinos also suffered atrocity from the occupation of American troops. Between February 4, 1899, and July 4, 1902, the Americans caused the death of more than 250,000 Filipino men, women, and children as indicated by history. The occupying troops were told the Filipinos were savages; they were no better than the American Indians. The Filipinos thought they had finally gotten away from Spanish brutality; however, they also suffered under American rule from the widespread torture, concentration camps, killing of disarmed prisoners of war (POW) and civilians. The ruthlessness of the American conquerors surpassed that of the Spaniards.

On one occasion, as confessed by one officer, while they were in reconnaissance, they passed through a village; the Filipinos lined up alongside the road and greeted the Americans. They tipped their hats and welcomed them with "Buenas dias los Señor Americanos." They said, "Good morning, Americans." The good American soldiers instead fired their guns upon the welcoming people and slaughtered them and ransacked the town. At a place known as Malabon, prior to the arrival of American troops, they bombarded the town, and then they went into the town, and any civilian they met were killed on the spot—men, women, and children. They found one Spanish mestiza woman; they raped her, taking turns, beginning with the officers and the enlisted last. A certain General gave the order that no prisoner would be taken. Several Filipinos approached U.S. troops with white flag. As soon as the Filipinos got close, they were all killed. One soldier wrote a letter to his parents, saying, "We sure have lots of fun here, we are shooting Filipinos like rabbits, by the hundreds or thousands." And the people back in States did not mind at all. Even President Theodore Roosevelt hailed the returning soldiers for their killing of thousands of civilians with the words "The bravery of American soldiers" who fought "for the triumph of civilization over the black chaos of savagery and barbarism." For the president, the extermination of hundreds of thousands of noncombatant civilians and defenseless POWs in the Philippines represented "the most glorious war in the nation's history." The cause of the killings and massacre of Filipinos was the order from the higher echelon, "No prisoners." The Filipinos were considered as savages on a level with American Indians. From the previous chapter, General Emilio Aguinaldo was captured and taken to Manila where he formally surrender the country; and on April 1901, Aguinaldo took an oath of allegiance to the United States of America. On April 19, 1901, Aguinaldo issued a proclamation appealing to the Filipinos to accept American sovereignty.

This ended the Filipino-American War.

CHAPTER 4

The Beginning Of Filipino-American Honeymoon

In 1935, the Philippines became the United States Commonwealth of the Philippines. The President was Manuel L. Quezon with its Vice President Sergio Osmeña. Free public education was introduced in the Philippines. Many soldiers were assigned to teach American English; later, they were replaced by civilian teachers coming from United States.

Streets were renamed after American states, such as Arkansas, California, Colorado, Dakota, Georgia, Florida, Indiana, Nebraska, Oregon, Pennsylvania, Tennessee, Texas, and Washington.

Universities started to sprout like a crop of mushrooms. The University of the Philippines was granted ten acres of land for its campus. Several universities sprouted in Taft Avenue. There were the Women's University, Normal College, De la Salle College, Ateneo de Manila, Mapua Institute of Technology, etc. By June 1900, Captain Albert Todd was named superintendent of the public schools in the entire Philippines. About one hundred thousand Filipino schoolchildren were attending schools. American civilian school teachers were sent to the Philippines to provide educational instruction. For the first time in the history of the world, a batch of six hundred teachers were transported to Manila. An act No. 74, which created the Department of Public Instruction, was to ensure to the people of the Philippines a system of free public schools. During the three hundred—year rule of the Spanish regime, no free schooling was provided to the people of the Philippines. Only the *illustrados* were given the opportunity for higher educations.

In 1901, the Philippine Normal School was established to provide instructions to Filipino teachers by American educators. All expenses were shouldered by the Philippines; none was coming from the United States. Charles Burke Elliot, who served in the Philippine Commission from 1910 to 1912, wrote in 1916, appealing to the U.S. Congress for monetary assistance, but his appeal fell on deaf ears.

After the introduction of the educational system, the transportation followed. Railway system came to existence, and the land and maritime transportation started growing as well. Communication throughout the island has also improved. The Philippine Commission passed an act No. 1, appropriating two million pesos for the construction of roads and bridges. The Spaniards built many roads but were just soft dirt, no gravel, and when monsoon season came, the roads were not passable. The Americans upgraded many roads that led to the improvement of the infrastructure program. The electric railway was constructed in Manila area known as tramvia. The railway system was extended all the way to the Bicol region, which the sugar growers used to transport the sugar cane to the processing company in nearby Manila. The interisland ferryboats connected Manila to other provinces.

The establishment of the Philippine Army began. Manuel L. Quezon, before assuming the presidency of the Philippine Commonwealth, worked out a system of national defense. On his visit to Washington, D.C., in 1935, he asked the U.S. Army Chief of Staff, General Douglas MacArthur, if the Philippines was defensible. Quezon brought the matter of the defense of the Philippines to President Franklin Delano Roosevelt and sought the services of the former Chief of Staff of the U.S. Armed Forces. President Roosevelt sent General Douglas MacArthur to the Philippines with Colonel Dwight D. Eisenhower and Colonel James B. Ord. At the request of President Manuel L. Quezon, the Philippine Army was established under the auspices of General Douglas MacArthur as Field Marshal. MacArthur gave Quezon some pointers on military science, which concluded that the Philippines may indeed "achieve a respectable defense and enjoy a reasonable safety if it is prepared and determined to repel attacks from foreign government." Quezon sought the help of the United States. President Manuel Quezon submitted before the legislature the first measure of his administration—the national defense program, which, among many other things, made military service compulsory to all Filipinos. On June 19, 1941, President Quezon pledged the loyalty of the Philippines to the United States, should the United States enter a war. The Philippines thus was aligned with the world democracy. That made the Philippines one of the prime targets associated in the plan to promote Japanese expansionism in Asia.

CHAPTER 5

Yesteryears

The Author and Presenter of This Historic Document

Kelly Samaco Medina (the author) was born about twelve o'clock to Carmen Samaco Medina in St. Paul Hospital, Intramuros, Manila, Philippines on October 25, 1931. As far as I can remember, we lived in Ermita, Manila. My father was a new graduate with a degree of Master of Science in Chemistry and was teaching at the University of the Philippines in Padre Faura, Manila.

When I was about four years old, our house was gutted by fire reportedly started by a Chinese restaurant owner. We moved to Viscara, Pasay, in a small nipa hut owned by Dr. Juan Salcedo, a professor at the University of the Philippines.

One early afternoon, my father took me to the Luneta Public Park to watch a parade. I was tagging along by his coattails. Suddenly I noticed I was not with my father anymore; I was tagging on somebody else's coat. The man noticed me, and then asked, "What are you doing here?"

I said, "I thought you are my father."

He inquired, "What's your father's name?"

I replied, "His name is Tatay."

He took me to a police station. A police officer asked me the same question, "What's your father's name?"

I said again, "Tatay."

"Your father's name?"

I said again, "My father's name is Tatay."

By the way, *Tatay* means dad (pronounced Tah tah i). Later my father found me in the police station, sitting on a chair, enjoying the ice cream given by a policeman. Upon seeing my dad, I was happy. I jumped off the chair and almost dropped the ice cream because of my excitement. My dad was so happy to be reunited with me; he hugged me and said, "Don't get lost again." We went home; this time he carried me to make sure I wouldn't get lost again.

After a brief stay in Viscara, my father joined the Philippine Army. He was commissioned as a Probationary Third Lieutenant, which required us to move to Sta. Mesa, Manila. This place was closer to Camp Murphy where my father was stationed. I enrolled in Padre Burgos Elementary School in Sta. Mesa. My father was promoted to the rank of first lieutenant in Chemical Warfare in 1936; we moved to Camp Murphy Officers Cottage after his transfer to the regular force of the Philippine Army. He was later promoted to the rank of Captain and became Company Commander of Company F, the Chemical Warfare Company.

My vivid memory of Camp Murphy as we entered it was that the camp was more of a pastoral setting. I noticed, standing before the camp, two water towers about twenty feet in diameter and forty feet high, painted yellow with black stripes around their circumference. On both sides of the main gate were two murals of Filipinos depicting their struggle for freedom. In the center was posted a sentry and on the right was a guardhouse. In the middle of the street was an island lined with needle-pine trees. At the end of the street was a huge grandstand with two cannons with spoke wheels and a pole bearing an American flag and a Filipino flag. Our car made a sudden right turn then, which enable me to see the officers' clubhouse.

We then turned to the left to see rows of cottages with nameplates under each mailbox to designate those who were occupying them. We stopped at cottage no. 48. It looked like a Southern state house with a big veranda. The cottage was painted white with green stripping. It had a garage, two big bedrooms, a bath between them, a dining room, and a living room. On top of the garage were quarters for servants.

We were introduced to our neighbors. Living on our right were Lieutenants Batongmalake and Ernesto Mata, on our left were Lieutenants Villaluz and Friedlander, and in front of us were Lieutenants Alberto Llanes and Jose Lucero and Captain Francisco Vargas. Located behind us were bigger houses reserved for higher rank officers, Colonel Mateo Capinpin and Colonel Basilio Vadez.

The street in front of our cottage led us to the Army Air Corps Base known as Zablan Air Field. The street was lined with *arateris* and *kaimito* trees. The driveway to the field was paved with kutcharita shrubs.

In the early mornings, we were entertained by plebes from the Air Corps doing their jogging every morning. To impress my mestiza cousin Marieta and Aunt Flora, this exercise was usually done in place double time. Our playmates were Junior Bert Llanes, Boy Lucero, Villaluz, Lucy Llanes, and Erlinda Llanes.

Ernesto, my younger brother, and I went to the same school in Sta. Mesa. My younger sister, Lettie, and young brother Junior went to kindergarten inside the Army compound. My uncles Buhay and Malacas, Aunt Flora, and cousin Marieta stayed with us. Uncle Buhay went to the University of the Philippines and studied medicine. Uncle Malacas also attended the same University and studied electrical engineering. Aunt Flora and Cousin Marieta went to Centro Escolar College. Our helpers were Teresita and Usting Root from Ilocos, and Liling from Visayas. My brothers and sisters were Ernesto (Erning), Florencio Junior (Unyoy), Leticia (Lettie), Isagani (Amang), Augusto (Usting), Nellie (Lallie), and Carmen (Baby). We were a big family under one roof. I did not know how Mother managed to cook and take care of all of us.

During this time, we had many events, like the day Nanay (Mom) decided to make us (Ernesto and myself) take the Metro City Bus instead of the school bus. Mom found out that taking the school bus was expensive, so we started to take the city bus, waiting for it outside the main gate of the compound. Mother gave us ten centavos for our bus fare and lunch. That money was enough for us then. Uncle Kario Inumerable would sometimes pick us up for lunch with him.

Ernesto and I were carried away one day, spending all the money we had on food, and next thing we knew, our bus fare was gone. We decided to walk not realizing the distance from school to our house was more than twenty miles, a long walk for eight—and seven-year-old boys. And it was getting dark. We started to find our way. In the meantime, our parents were getting worried. Their two boys were missing. The whole Philippine

Army was alerted to find us. Fortunately, an army truck stopped to give us a lift. When we asked the driver to take us to Camp Murphy, he expressed surprise at our request. He said, "Aha! So you are the two boys the whole army is looking for. I had better take you home right now."

Our parents were so much relieved to see us. We got our spanking on the butt—a common punishment back then. My dad would order us to lie on our belly on the floor, then he would give us three slashes on our butts. We became so smart. Before we received our spanking, we would insert a cardboard inside our pants. Dad soon found out that we put a cardboard inside our pants, so he ordered us to remove our pants and spank us on our naked butts.

We, the boys from Camp Murphy officers' cottages, were just too restless. We would climb the papaya trees, pick their fruits, peel them, and eat them. Sometimes we would climb the arateris tree, playing around like young monkeys. While playing around the muddy pond one day, Ernesto and I pushed Lassie, a bully, into it. He came out wet and had mud all over him. My father was told about this, and again he gave us three lashes on our butts and scolded us. Lassie's father happened to be the Commanding Officer of Camp Murphy, Colonel Basilio Valdez. Our playmates were Alberto Llanes Jr., Boy Lucero, Junior Luna, Lucy and Linda Llanes and a Villaluz.

Tatay came home one day, wearing his sharp military uniform. He wore a Stetson hat with blue tussles in front of the rim, khaki breaches with thin blue piping along the side of both legs, a Sam Brown belt over his shoulder and around his waist, and a saber hanging by his left waist. He wore a well-polished high brown cavalry boots. His insignias and belt buckle were immaculately shined. Dad brought home some gas mask that needed fixing. I remember him using a rubber glue, the smell of which to this day still gets to me. He taught Mom how to use the gas mask. "Protection against poison gas attack," he assured her.

We would watch the officers and soldiers do military exercises and mock wars in front of our houses once a week. They would mostly run and jump into ditches with their Springfield rifles. They were practicing to prepare them for war. On Saturdays, they would have a military parade. On one occasion, I saw General Douglas MacArthur with his Chief of Staff, Colonel Dwight Eisenhower, and the President of the Philippines, Manuel L. Quezon. They were on the grandstand, reviewing the military parade. The soldiers marched in precision with the band of First Lieutenant Carino leading the formation, playing "Stars and Stripe Forever." Almost every day, we would hear the marching band rehearsal led by First Lieutenant Carino.

His favorite compositions seemed to be John Phillip Sousas' "Washington Post March," "King Cotton March," "El Capitan," and other tunes. A loud, blaring trumpet sound would awake us to signal reveille in the morning and the solemn sound of taps about nine o'clock at night.

The band would go around the army compound and serenade us during the holidays. This would go on until New Year's Day. On Christmas Day, Mom and Dad would bring us children to the clubhouse to party. There would be many gifts surrounding a Christmas tree, and when a raffle of tickets was held one time, I won a big basket full of goodies.

The color of the basket—red and green—seemed to attract me. In the basket were apples, pears, Sunkist oranges, grapes, century pears, and lots of nuts and toys. The toys were made in Japan, how ironic that in a few months, we would hate those toys made in Japan. After playing with the airplane, I disassembled it one time, removing its wings and tail then reassembling it to look like a cannon (ingenious of my talents).

Mom and Dad would take us children to a Chinese restaurant on some weekends. Dad's favorite then was Mamon Luk whose specialty was *Mami* (noodles soup) and *siopao* (big-size dumpling). Sometimes, Mom and Dad would go out by themselves. On their way back home, they would always carry with them a bagful of *hopia* (Chinese pastry); they would just wake us up to eat it.

One weekend, the whole family went to Binakayan, Kawit, Cavite, to Nanay's aunt (Lola Juana Agco). There we met our uncles, Remy and Eking, and Aunt Luz and Luming. We had a fun time eating oysters and *kapis* (seashell); on our way back, we stopped to visit Mom's cousins, the Tulaos. They gave us a big bottle of *patis* (fish sauce). Dad handed it to me to carry. When we arrived at the gate of Camp Murphy, the bottle slipped off from my grip and fell on the concrete. The bottle broke, and the whole place stunk because of the patis. The main gate had to be washed down that evening. The smell was unbearable. Tatay scolded me for not holding it tightly. That was a special gift from Mom's relative.

CHAPTER 6

Japanese Army And Navy Disagreement To Engage In War With America

As early as 1928, the Japanese government and its military command disagreed about plans to attack the bases of United States, Great Britain, and the Netherlands in Southeast Asia. Several attempts were made by the civil government, but it could not come up with a better agreement. The Japanese Army occupying China resisted withdrawal from their occupied area. The Japanese Army violated several orders from the civil government and, instead, occupied a large portion of northern China. There was also an abuse of power by the *kempetai* (military police). Many Chinese male of military age were murdered then used as dummies for bayonet practice, and women and girls were raped then murdered. The Japanese Army had the intention of going to war against the United States; however, both the Civil Government and the Navy High Command did not agree with the army. Prime Minister Prince Konoye and the Emperor disagreed with the army. The Navy Combined Forces also disagreed. Admiral Isoroku Yamamoto, was a graduate of Harvard University and had been a Naval Attaché in Washington. He had traveled widely in the United States and had known the extent of the industrial might of the United States.

He believed that if Japan attacked the United States, it could not prolong the war for an extended period because Japan did not have the industrial power that the United States possesses. He was, however, under order from the Prime Minister Hideki Tojo. Admiral Isoroku Yamamoto was a brilliant planner, tactician, and strategist. Because of his pro-American attitude and the fear of assassination by the ultranationalist, he was sent to sea. He was ordered to develop a plan, with the help of Commander Genda, for the attack on Pearl Harbor while negotiations were ongoing in Washington and Japan. The negotiation was carried on between Secretary of State Hull and Japanese Ambassador Nomora, a retired navy admiral. Yamamoto, even against his will, had to continue to develop a plan to attack America under pressure of Prime Minister Hideki Tojo. Tojo's plan was to attack the Southeast Asian countries, especially those under the ABCD powers or America, Britain, China, and Dutch. And after they have occupied those countries, they planned to establish the Greater East Asia Co-prosperity Sphere—"Asia for Asian." Because of the economic blockage by the ABCD, Japan was experiencing hard living, and poverty was spreading all over Japan. They were being strangled economically, and this was coupled with the racial discrimination of the United States against Japanese immigrants. Japan had to have mineral resources, oil, and other by-products. The United States did not trust the Japanese because of the occupation of Manchuria and China and also of Korea. The United States believed that the Japanese's intention to have continued access to the natural resources of other Asian countries was to further support their expansion in all of Asia.

Prime Minister Hideki Tojo of Japan.
Japanese Army in at ease.

While Yamamoto was in the process of making the plans, he encountered several problems with the planned use of torpedo bombers. The spies in Hawaii reported that the harbor water was shallow; the torpedoes, dropped from the bombers, would hit the bottom. A Japanese designer in Yokosuka Naval Shipyard came up with a design to improve the torpedo's stability and buoyancy so that it would not hit the bottom by adding a fin stabilizer made of wood. They secretly conducted a mock attack using Kagoshima Harbor as Pearl Harbor. After several dry runs over Kagoshima, their conclusion was that they would enjoy an about 80 percent success in attacking Pearl Harbor.

To ensure success in Southeast Asia, they had a mock landing on the island of Hainan. They landed twenty thousand soldiers on Hainan. They were very successful, which strengthened the possibility of going to war then than at any time before. If they missed this chance, there would not be another, and Japan would become a third-class nation.

While at the same time, they had Ambassador Nomura continue negotiation with the Secretary of State Hull who really did not trust Nomura. U.S. naval intelligence had intercepted the message from Tokyo advising the Embassy to start burning secret documents and destroying the decoder. President Franklin D. Roosevelt sent a message to Emperor Hirohito urging peace between the two countries. That message did not get to Emperor Hirohito on time due to many red tapes along the way. Foreign Minister Togo and Prime Minister Tojo said that the message from President Roosevelt was too late. General MacArthur and Admiral Hart of the Asiatic Fleet were informed of the oncoming war with Japan, but this was put aside. There was mass confusion in the Japanese Embassy and in Washington, D.C., as well. The last item for negotiation from Tokyo needed to be decoded and translated into English, but it took the translator and decoder a long time. Ambassador Nomura could not wait for the translator to finish and yanked the paper from the typewriter and took it with him to Secretary Hull to read before giving it to President Roosevelt. By the time Secretary Hull received the last item for negotiation, the attack on Pearl Harbor was over. Ambassador Nomura did not have any knowledge that the Combined Japanese Forces had already attacked Pearl Harbor. Colonel Braton's sense that the part from Tokyo must be submitted to Washington by 1:00 PM. made him feel that America would be attacked soon. He tried to call General Marshall, the Chief of Staff, but General Marshall had left home for his daily horseback ride. After General Marshall arrived home, the message was given to him by

Sergeant Aguirre. General Marshall phoned Colonel Braton and inquired about the sudden phone call. Colonel Braton could not fully explain his hunch about the possibility of Japan attacking the United States. General Marshall was about to call to warn Admiral Kimmel about the possible Japanese attack but changed his mind, thinking there was no point in warning Admiral Kimmel because he had already warned Admiral Kimmel in late November.

While the negotiations were going on, the Combined Fleet Kido Butai was underway to Hawaiian Islands. The Kido Butai slipped off the launching undetected; it was about two hundred miles off Pearl Harbor. Admiral Kusaka in his flagship, *Akagi*, ordered that the Z flag be raised. The crew from the other carrier *Kaga*, upon seeing this signal, raised their own. Everybody was very excited that morning. Later, the triangular flag was raised, which signaled ready for take off. The pilots were in their cockpit, waiting for the signal. Lieutenant Shiga wanted to be the first to be airborne, so he took off without even giving a salute to his commander; but when he was in the air, he found in dismay that Lt. Commander Shigeru Itaya was in the air ahead of him. All the fighter planes were airborne. Then the medium-high level bombers, led by Squadron leader Heijiro Abe, took air from *Soryu* right behind the fighter planes. They were followed by Aichi Type 99 dive bombers and Najima Type 97 torpedo bombers under squadron leader Hirata Matsumura, which took off from the carrier *Hiryu*. The launch took only fifteen minutes to complete. Only one zero did not make the flight; it crashed during takeoff. They leveled off at thirteen thousand feet on their way to their target—the Pearl Harbor.

In Pearl Harbor, it was about 6:30 AM. The antisubmarine net was opened to let the target ship *Antares* into the harbor. Just outside the harbor, the destroyer USS *Ward* was underway. The skipper, a young Lieutenant William Outerbridge, was roused from his bunk. Outerbridge saw something unusual that looked like a submarine's conning tower and right away called for general quarters. He sighted a small submarine 1,500 yards off the starboard quarter and ordered to shoot at point-blank range; the number one gun fired and missed, but the number three fired and hit the conning tower. Then the skipper ordered to drop four depth charges. He then radioed the Fourteenth Naval district with the following: "WE HAVE DROPPED DEPTH CHARGES ON SUB OPERATING IN DEFENSIVE AREA." The message was ignored because it was not strong enough to be considered a serious matter. Again, they sent another radio message after two minutes later: "WE HAVE ATTACKED FIRED UPON AND DROPPED DEPTH CHARGES UPON SUBMARINE OPERATING IN DEFENSIVE AREA." There was a delay in decoding the second message; however, the second message was received by Admiral Kimmel's Chief of Staff, John B. Earle, at 7:12 AM. Few minutes later, Admiral Claude C. Bloch read it and said, "What do you think about it?" Admiral Earle was dubious and, complaining, he said, "We get so many of these false sightings. We can't go off half-cocked." The reason for this was that several months before, there were several reports of submarine sighting; they were verified, but they were all false reports. At almost the same moment, the advanced radar facilities at Kahuku point observed a large aircraft on its way, approaching Oahu. Private George Elliott, Jr., manning the radar, reported the sighting to his counterpart, Private Joseph Lockard of the 515th Signal Aircraft Warning Service, who was more knowledgeable in determining the images. They immediately reported their findings to the Information Center at Fort Shaftner but could not find anyone on duty except a pilot named Kermit Tyler. When told of the large number of aircraft on their way to Oahu, Tyler replied, "Don't worry about it," and hung up. Everyone on the island knew of the incoming flying fortress coming from California—the reason they ignored the report of the approaching danger. A Japanese seaplane was making a final routine check in Lahaina for any American ship in Lahaina and another flying over Pearl Harbor. No one noticed the planes flying above them that morning. The seaplane even radioed back to Kido Butai the findings: "ENEMY'S FLEET NOT AT LAHAINA 0305."

Another seaplane flying above Pearl Harbor reported, "ENEMY'S FLEET IN PEARL HARBOR."

These two message were the most delightful messages Admiral Kusaka had been waiting for.

At the same time, Foreign Minister Togo had just arrived at the Palace grounds, saying to himself, "It is going to be a fine day." The Foreign Minister was ushered into the Emperor's presence. At that time, it was almost the same time Nomura and Kurusu were supposed to meet Secretary Hull. Togo read before the Emperor the message from President Roosevelt and the proposed draft of his reply, which at that moment, Togo thought reflected "a noble feeling of brotherhood with all people."

Attack on Pearl Harbor
December 7, 1941

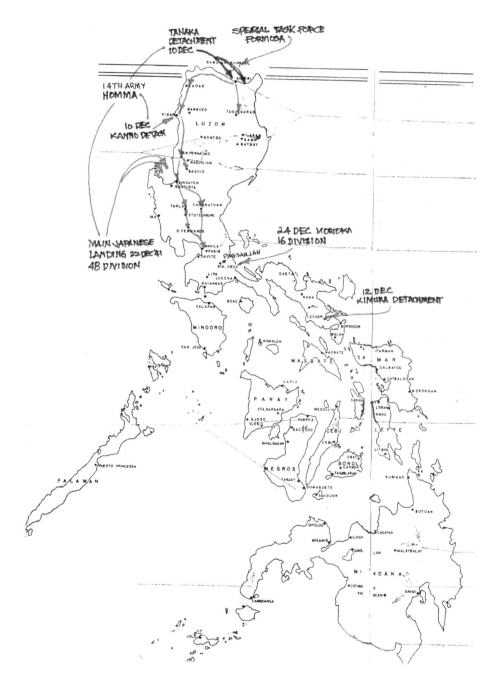

Japanese landings in the Philippines

CHAPTER 7

When Rising Sun Was Flying Over
In The Philippine Sky

Dad was promoted to Captain in Chemical Warfare Service and was inducted into the United States Army Forces in the Far East (USAFFE) in September 1941. In November 1941, Dad was transferred to the 101st Infantry Division in Malaybalay, Mindanao, serving under Brigadier General Joseph Vachon, U.S. Army. Our family had to vacate our cottage in Camp Murphy to transfer to Mindanao. The supposed transfer was a blessing in disguise that forced us to move to an apartment in Park Avenue, Pasay City, owned by Mr. Galves. The camp would be bombed and strafed by the Japanese Air Force a few weeks later.

JAPANESE AIR

JAPANESE NAVY AIR POWER

A movie house near our apartment was showing a matinee show titled *The Fighting 69th* that starred James Cagney. We wanted to see the movie, but lack of money prevented us from doing so. We asked Mom for some movie money but were turned down. We then looked around for something to sell to have some movie money. We found a ten-foot one-inch water pipe lying at the back of our apartment. Without hesitation or permission, we took it, dragged it to the nearest junkyard, and sold it for ten centavos. This money was enough for Ernesto and me to enter the movie house. Looking around, we saw Onyoy (Jun), our younger brother, with a sad face; he also wanted to go with us. We felt sorry for him; we did not have enough money to bring him with us. We told him to tag along behind the old man in front of us. That was what he did, and the ticket teller did not notice him holding the tailcoat of the old man. We distracted the teller by making all kinds of noises, and she was busy telling us to keep quiet. We stopped as soon as Onyoy got into the movie house; he waited for us to get in and then ran to our side to watch the movie. That was the last one we saw until the liberation of the Philippines from Japan.

Japanese Air Force attack on Pearl Harbor
December 7, 1941

We were to join Dad in Bukidnon, Mindanao, and our stay in Park Avenue was supposed to be temporary. While waiting for our transportation to take us south, Ernesto and I enrolled in Pasay Elementary School. I was in fourth grade and Ernesto in third. Between classes, we were taught to go under the school building, a practice drill for air raid. We heard about the possibility of the Japanese attacking us. In fact, they had already occupied a large portion of China. They had also amassed a huge number of their military forces in Formosa (now Taiwan).

On December 7, 1941, at eight in the morning, while the Americans were enjoying the early sun and recuperating from the previous night and others were getting ready for Sunday church services, the Japanese Imperial Air Forces attacked Pearl Harbor. Fifty-nine years later, I have a Japanese wife named Etsuko, and she told me her uncle was one of the pilots who made the attack on Pearl Harbor. He was killed in action—shot down by the American antiaircraft gun and died instantly. At the same time across the Pacific, a similar attack was made in the Philippines.

Japanese Marines boarding landing craft off Lingayen gulf

Japanese landing forces in Bataan

A building in Manila when under attack by U.S Forces.

In the morning of December 8, 1941, Mom was packing our clothes and dishware for our trip to Mindanao. My two uncles, Manong Buhay and Tio Salus, suddenly showed up. Both looked worried; they were pale and did not know how to start and what to say. Looking at them, Mom was thinking maybe they came over to help her pack our belongings. She was unaware of what was going on. Mom continued her packing, happy, thinking we would soon be reunited with my father.

Manong Buhay asked Mom, "What are you doing?"

Happily Mom replied, "I am packing our belongings for our trip to join Florencio in Mindanao."

Uncle Salus, who looked very much like a Japanese, told Mom, "You are not going anywhere at this time. The ship SS *Corregidor* that you are going to take to Mindanao was sunk in Manila Bay, the ship was hit by a floating mine, and it exploded and sunk right in the bay."

"Don't you know that there is a war going on?" he continued. "The Japanese are bombing Nichols Airfield [now Villamor], Camp Murphy in Rizal City, Camp John Hay in Baguio City, Clark Air Force Base in Angeles, Pampanga, and Fort Stotsenburg in Tarlac, and Camp O'Donnell in Cabanatuan, Nueva Ecija." Mom exclaimed, "What shall I do now?"

Tio Salus advised her "to go to Mindoro where it is much safer."

However, Mom became upset that she could not make up her mind whether to pack or not. She remembered from an indoctrination class she had attended with Dad at Camp Murphy that she and our family of eight dependents had to go to an evacuation center, and the nearest one was in Pangsanjan, Laguna. Mom had to go along with the instructions Dad gave her a few days before he left for his new duty station because while Dad was at Camp Murphy, they went to an indoctrination class. Mom then continued packing, not for Mindanao, but for the nearest evacuation center. Instead, she packed light baggage, which included clothing and some snacks. Mom, now well-informed of what to do, decided to evacuate to Pagsanjan, Laguna, which was planned in the first place. Manuel Uy, a Sweepstake game owner, was her closet relative in Manila, living in Trece de Agosto in Paco, Manila, across the train station. We moved to his house because it was close to the train station. While waiting for the train that would take us out of Manila, we experienced the first aerial attack and bombing of the city of Manila. There was no air raid shelter close by to protect us from the bombing. We heard the air raid siren, no place to hide but under the table.

On December 26, 1941, at the advice of President Quezon, MacArthur declared the city of Manila an open city to spare it from further destruction and death caused by military operations. The Japanese Air Force continued on bombing the city anyway.

The city was not ready for aerial attack. There was chaos all over the city with everyone looking for the nearest air raid shelter. There was no air raid shelter close by to protect us from the bombing. After the aerial attack, people of all ages ransacked and looted the Chinese and Japanese stores for food or anything useful. They took anything their hands could reach. After several days of waiting, the train finally arrived. We were in a hurry to get out of the city because of the constant bombing of the city.

Japanese Infantry about to enter Manila

At the time that the bombing was going on, two Filipino Air Corps pilots, Lieutenant Jose Gozar and Captain Jesus Villamor, ran to their planes and intercepted the mighty Japanese Air Force. With their obsolete planes, they were, of course, no match for the modern Japanese aircraft. They tried to shoot them, but to no avail. The enemy outmaneuvered them in the dogfight. They were forced to return to their base Zablan. Lieutenant Jose Gozar, PAC, could not outmaneuver the fast Japanese Zero and was shot down during the dogfight; he was killed. Captain Jesus Villamor escaped

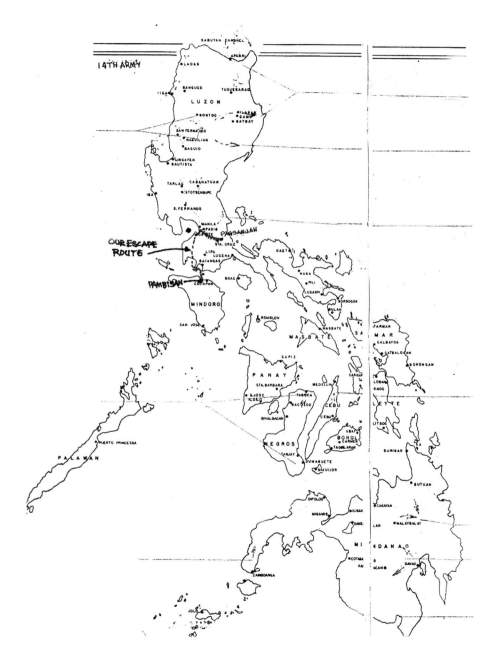

Escape route from Manila and Mindoro island

and made his way to Australia where he continued his fight against the Japanese as an Intelligence Officer of the U.S. Army. He slipped back to the Philippines to gather information on the Japanese strength, positions, and naval movement and reported the same to the Headquarters of the Supreme Allied Commander. He went to Manila, Mindanao, Panay, Negros, and Mindoro under a different name. Informed of his presence, the Japanese began to hunt him. His vital intelligence reports contributed to the successful liberation of the Philippines.

Meanwhile, back in Manila, the train was packed full when it arrived in Paco Station. It did not take us long to board the train and load the passenger car. It was survival of the fittest. Thank God, with the help of our helpers, Usting Root and Teresita, we made it on board, all eight children and Mom. Then we were very happy to get out of Manila because of that constant bombing of the city, especially since there was no place to hide and no air raid shelter. I was scared. I hid under the table with my butt out, as I remember the incident.

On the train, we traveled across the plains and coconut plantations. We were very fortunate the enemy planes did not spot or attack us on our way to Pagsanjan. When we arrived in Pagsanjan, Ate Flora (Dad's youngest sister) and Manong Kiko, her husband, met us at the train station. Upon arriving in Pagsanjan, my job was to muster all my siblings to ensure everybody was accounted for safely. Manong Kiko, an engineer for the Caliraya Hydroelectric Plant in Pagsanjan, Laguna, gave us a hand to assist us in every way he could. It was a very fortunate and good time for us to have them to give us assistance, especially in a strange place and in a confusing situation. While there, I listened to the radio, and I heard that the Japanese landed in Lingayen Gulf and in Aparri, the northernmost part of Luzon, which was in very close proximity to Formosa. Formosa was a Japanese territory; it became Japan's territory after China fell to Japan. The island became Japan's military staging or jumping board in the invasion of several Southeast Asian nations.

At the time, Japan insisted that the Southeast Asian countries become a part of the Co-prosperity Sphere of which Japan would be the hub or center of contact connections. Japan made this move because of the economic tightening of the ABCD or America, Britain, China, and Dutch alliance. Japan had to control the Southeast Asian nations in order to survive. These Southeast Asian nations including the Philippines were under the Western powers of America: India, Hong Kong, Burma, and Borneo of Britain; China of China; Indonesia of Netherlands; and Indochina of France.

Two Japanese forces located and coming from NORTH AND south of Manila were bivouacked and in preparation to enter the city on the following day.

Along with the news, I listened to Bing Crosby's "Because of You." It was meaningful to me. We stayed in Pagsanjan for several days when Mom heard of the approaching danger of the Japanese landings in Atimonan, Tayabas (now Quezon). She was thankful for making a quick decision to go to Mindoro via Manila, Cavite, and Batangas. By the time we reached Manila, the Japanese had occupied the city of Manila without shooting a single shot. Manila, being an open city (safety zone) with no protection, was no challenge. The Japanese Imperial Army had secured towns and cities from Aparri in the north, Lingayen Gulf in the west on December 23, 1941, Atimonan in the east, and Davao in the south; and Bataan and Corregidor were still fighting. We returned to our apartment on Park Avenue. The city was in ruins because of air raid. The Japanese Imperial Army occupied the city of Manila on January 2, 1942, without resistance from either the Philippine Army or U.S. Army.

Because the Americans gave Europe priority and sent no support to the Philippines, the Philippines lost the battle against the superior Japanese invading forces. Brigadier General Vicente Lim, in charge of seventy-four thousand Filipino officers and men and military of the Forty-first Division and known as the Rock of Bataan, was in the frontline of the battlefield. Out of the seventy-eight thousand Filipino-American troops in Bataan, only four thousand were Americans, and they were at the rear as reserves. Brigadier General Vicente Lim was the first Filipino to graduate from West Point; his classmate was former President Dwight Eisenhower in 1914. In 1941, the defending forces were losing ground; Bataan and Corregidor were low on provisions, armaments, medicines, and water. Both fronts were suffering from heavy casualties that made it impossible to defend both Bataan and Corregidor. Corregidor was a dead island; the constant bombing by superior Japanese Air Force and pounding from the Japanese Imperial Navy made it impossible to stay above ground. They stayed in Malinta Tunnel, with a well-furnished hospital made for the purpose and where military strategic planning operations were held. The Japanese had control of air, sea, and ground movements. With no further military assistance coming from United States, President Roosevelt ordered General MacArthur to vacate the island fortress. On March 11, 1942, General MacArthur, his family, and few staff officers were forced to evacuate to Australia by Torpedo Boat under cover of darkness through Mindanao where they took a plane, which took them to Australia. The Commonwealth of the Philippines President Manuel L. Quezon, Vice President Sergio Osmeña, General Carlos P. Romulo, and their immediate families left Corregidor on board a submarine to form a government in exile in the United States. Left behind were Dr. Jose P. Laurel, Associate Chief Justice Abad Santos, Statesman Camilo Osias, General Mateo Capinpin, General Vicente Lim, General Manuel Roxas, Statesmen Francisco, Jose Yulo, Rafael Alunan, Quintin Paredes, Vicente Madrigal, Pio Duran, Benigno Aquino, Major General Edward P. King, and Army General Jonathan Wainwright.

Fall of Corregidor
Surrender of Malinta Tunnel

On the night of March 9, 1942, before General MacArthur left Corregidor, he sent word through his Chief of Staff for his First Corps commander and successor, Major General Jonathan M. Wainwright, to report to him at Malinta Tunnel the next morning. General Jonathan Wainwright, like MacArthur, had deep roots in the American army. His father, too, was a senior military man and a graduate of West Point who served many years as a cavalryman at frontier posts in the west. The senior Wainwrights, father and grandfather, served on the staff of Major General

Arthur MacArthur in the Philippines. The son, newly commissioned Second Lieutenant Wainwright, followed his father into cavalry. He served in a succession of isolated western posts before being sent to the Philippines in 1909. Like General MacArthur, the Second Lieutenant first experienced combat against the Moro rebels in the islands. After a brief tour of duty in Europe, he was sent to the Philippines in October 1940 to take command of the Philippine Division. Soon after General Wainwright moved over to Corregidor, the Japanese launched a major offensive on Bataan. Fifty thousand fresh Japanese troops stepped off on April 3, 1942. Though the remaining seventy-eight Filipino-American defenders in Bataan fought as valiantly as they could with limited supplies at their disposal, it was all in vain. On the same day, General Masaharu Homma, in commemoration of the Ancient Japanese Emperor Jimmu Tennohika Day, launched his total strength against the Filipino-American forces in Bataan. The Japanese Infantry and naval and air force swept through the Filipino-American lines, supported by heavy artillery and tanks. The Japanese forces had complete control of the battleground. The American and Filipino forces were suffering from hunger, disease, and fatigue, which eroded the strength and the will to fight. On April 9, 1943, against General Wainwright's expressed orders, Bataan's commander, Major General Edward P. King, surrendered his forces to General Homma. When Wainwright learned of the move, he visibly slumped at his desk. He wired the sad news to MacArthur and Marshall. After MacArthur's staff arrived in Australia in March 1942, radio contact was maintained with Corregidor for a short time. After the Fall of Corregidor, all communications with the Philippines was cut off except for a radio station operated by Lieutenant Colonel Nakar Guillermo of the Philippine Army from Nueva Ecija.

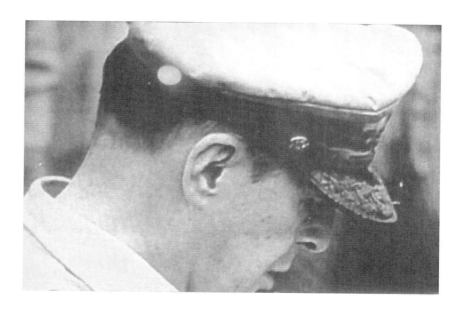

General Douglas MacArthur reading his last message to
American and Filipino soldiers before leaving Corregidor.

General MacArthur with his staff walking toward their PT
Boat that will take them to Australia.

General MacArthur reading a radio message with one of his staff officer looking on.

Some members of Philippine scout

On the night of December 7 in Manila, the Twenty-seventh Bombardment Group was giving a party in honor of Major General Lewis H. Brereton, commander of Far East Air Force that General MacArthur recently established. One of Admiral Hart's staff commented that it won't be long until the shooting would start. Brereton was feeling very uneasy and, as a precaution, put his airfield in combat alert. In Clark Field, sixteen flying fortresses were lined up. General Brereton suggested to General MacArthur to authorize him to bomb Formosa. MacArthur declined the suggestion, saying that the United States would be tagged as an aggressor. General Brereton said the Japanese had made their first attack. General MacArthur still declined the idea of bombing Formosa. The same day, prime minister Churchill arrived in Washington to confer with President Roosevelt about the Japanese concentrating a large military force in Formosa; the U.S. Navy submarine *Sting Ray* sighted the Japanese Navy consisting of eighty-five troop transports. Transportation was in the coastal shore of the Philippines in Lingayen, Pangasinan, awaiting orders to invade the Philippines. This was reported to General MacArthur to alert him of the approaching Japanese Imperial invasion forces led by General Masaharu Homma, an army commander. General Homma was an amateur playwright who had been, for a long time, against the war and attack on America. General Homma had spent many years with the British, including service in France in 1918 with the British Expeditionary Force of which he had a deep respect of the capability of the Western countries in war. Even after the Fall of Nanking, he wrote a book about the ruthless behavior toward the conquered civilians; he declared that "unless peace is achieved immediately it will be disastrous." He confided to his friend, General Muto, that Tojo would be a poor prime minister.

At 2:00 AM of December 22, he had his 43,110 battle-harden troops start landing. But it took the invading forces two and a half hours to load the battalion of infantry and a battalion of mountain artillery to land. On the beach, they found there was no resistance. By midmorning, they had established their command post; there was a light resistance from the lone Filipino battalion. By late in the afternoon, all the army and half of the tank forces were ashore and on the move toward south of Manila. General MacArthur, upon learning about the situation in Lingayen, sent a message to General Marshall for aerial support but was denied; the response was that it was impossible according to the navy and suggested to rely on the planes already ferried to Brisbane in Australia. After the attack in Clark Field, only four remaining flying fortresses were available to fly; they dropped a one-hundred-pound bomb and then turned south to Australia. The Filipino defenders, having only a few weeks of military training, had no knowledge in combat. They only knew how to use the outdated bolt-action Enfield rifles. They broke and fled, leaving the supporting artillery unprotected. General Jonathan Wainwright, the commander of all forces north of Luzon, phoned General MacArthur, requesting to withdraw behind the Agno River. MacArthur, realizing he had no navy or air support, agreed with Wainwright and established Filipino-American forces in Bataan Peninsula because the enemy landings could not be contained. And the defenders would hold out for six months until the reinforcement from the United States arrived. The next morning, the situation turned to worse; the Japanese had landed a giant pincer from twenty-four Japanese troop transport at Lamon Bay, southeast of Manila; almost ten thousand men of the Sixteenth Division advanced toward Manila. With the Japanese getting closer to Manila, MacArthur moved his headquarters to Malinta Tunnel in Corregidor Island under cover of darkness.

At Malacañan Palace, President Quezon summoned his executive secretary, Jorge Vargas, and Jose P. Laurel to make a sacrifice without a parallel for the good of the people and said, "You two will remain here and deal with the Japanese." He and vice president Osmeña would join MacArthur in Corregidor. However, Laurel protested, saying, "The people will call me a collaborator." He broke down and begged for permission to accompany Quezon to Corregidor. But Quezon insisted Laurel that it was his duty. Someone had to protect the people from the Japanese.

Meanwhile, there was mass confusion outside on the streets—army trucks going northeast to Bataan and Pambusco, a bus fighting its way south to Manila. Many arms, food, and medical provisions for Bataan were stranded along the way. There was no police or military police around to control the traffic. Smoke was all over Manila; the Pandacan oil field and the army and navy installation were all ablaze. At about five forty-five, the three battalions of the Forty-eight Division were entering Manila from the north. They were greeted with silence by Filipinos. The cheers were coming from the released Japanese from interment.

Across the bay, MacArthur was still holding out Corregidor. Malinta Tunnel, which was made from a solid granite inside the tunnel, can withstand bombs from above. The tunnel had a hospital and other supplies needed to sustain for six months. In Bataan on the night of January 5, General Nara—a stocky middle-aged man—led his troops toward the front on foot. Lieutenant General Akira Nara had spent many years in the United States, attended Amherst College as a classmate of President Coolidges's son, and graduated from Infantry School in Fort Benning, Georgia. They approached Bataan, crammed with fifteen thousand Americans and sixty-five thousand Filipino troops. Ten thousand of which were the elite Philippine Division, and the rest were nothing but ill-trained and ill-equipped group. On January 13, President Quezon sent a cablegram to President Roosevelt through MacArthur complaining that President Roosevelt failed to send reinforcement to the Philippines. His indignation carried over an accompanying note to MacArthur.

> Has it already been decided in Washington that the Philippine front is of no importance as far as the final result of the war is concerned and that, therefore, so help can be expected here in the immediate future, or at least before, the power of resistance is exhausted? If so, I want to know, because I have my own responsibility to my countrymen . . .

> I want to decide to my own mind whether there is justification for allowing all these men to be killed when for the final outcome of the war the shedding of their blood may be wholly unnecessary. It seems that Washington does not fully realize our situation nor the feelings which apparent neglect of our safety and welfare have engendered in the heart of the people here . . .

In Corregidor, President Quezon in his wheelchair was listening to the radio broadcast from U.S. in mounting fury as Roosevelt told radio audience how thousands of aircraft would soon be on their way to the battlefront in Europe.

Quezon pointed out the smoke rising in the mainland. He said, "For my thirty years, I have worked and hoped for my people. Now they burn and die for a flag that could not protect them. Nombre por Dios y todos los santos! I cannot stand this sinverguenza [scoundrel] is boosting of? How American writhe in anguish at the fate of a distant cousin while a daughter is being raped in the back room!"

He even go by suggesting to MacArthur, "Perhaps my presence on Corregidor is not of value. Why don't I go to Manila and become a prisoner of war?" MacArthur thought that such a surrender would be misinterpreted abroad. "I don't care what the outsiders think," Quezon snapped, but agreed to think it over.

That night, Second Lieutenant Antonio Aquino, eldest son of Benigno Aquino, the Speaker of the House in Philippine Congress, with the aid of ping-pong balls tied around his body, swam across the bay from Bataan to Corregidor and reported to President Quezon that there was a friction between the American and Filipino soldiers because the American supply officers gave a very limited ration to the Filipino soldiers. He said, "We eat only salmon and sardines. One can per day for thirty men, twice a day."

President Quezon was enraged upon hearing the sad news. He summoned his cabinet and said he would ask Roosevelt to let him issue a manifesto requesting the United States to grant absolute independence to the Philippines. He would then demobilize the Philippine Army and declare the Philippines neutral. Consequently, both the United States and Japan would withdraw their armies. However, Vice President Osmeña tried to point out the consequences of such an action in Washington, but Quezon could not be persuaded. Quezon was very much enraged that he kept on coughing, which was caused by severe tuberculosis. Osmeña reluctantly approved sending the message to Roosevelt without having MacArthur know about it. MacArthur, not only pass but rankled by his suspicion that Roosevelt and Marshall in particular had let him down. He, therefore, supported Quezon's message to Washington. "There is no denying that we are nearly done," he wrote. Quezon's plan "might offer the best possible solution of what is about to be disastrous debacle." With this, MacArthur was risking his military career. Marshall was dismayed that MacArthur "went more than halfway toward supporting Quezon's position." Roosevelt's reaction was unequivocal. "We can't do this at all," he told Marshall and Stimson, the secretary of war. The Chief of Staff had entertained some doubt about Roosevelt's leadership. The President's firm decision convinced him that he was after all a "great man." Roosevelt immediately informed Quezon that seventy-nine thousand troops would leave for the Pacific front, almost four times the number heading to Europe. Most of the planes were also bound for Southeast Asia.

Roosevelt, while rejecting Quezon's proposal as unacceptable to America, however, gave his word that no matter what Quezon did, the United States would never abandon the Philippines.

So long as the flag of the U.S. flies on Filipino soil . . . It will be defended by our own men to the death. Whatever happens to present American garrison we shall not relax our efforts until the forces which are now marshalling outside the Philippines return to the Philippines and drive out the last remnant of the invaders from your soil.

This message overwhelmed Quezon. He swore to himself and God that as long as he lived, he would stand by America regardless of the consequences to his people or himself. MacArthur received a more direct reply from Roosevelt.

The duty and the necessity of resisting Japanese aggression to the last transcends in importance any other obligation now facing us in the Philippines . . . I particularly request that you proceed rapidly to the organization of your forces and your defenses so as to make your resistance as effective as circumstances will permit and as prolonged as humanly possible.

This meant that the Philippines was now a lost cause, and MacArthur's valor was reduced to a symbol of resistance. He, however, replied that he would fight to the end and to the destruction on Bataan and then Corregidor, making them names for Americans to remember forever.

I have not the slightest intention in the world of surrendering or capitulating the Filipino element of my command . . . there has never been the slightest wavering among the troops.

This message was an exaggeration; it was truer than it had been a few weeks earlier. The soldiers were riddled by dysentery and malaria, and their uniforms in tatters. The half-staved men of Bataan were full of light and confidence. The Japanese had been held, and Filipino recruits who had fled in Lingayen Gulf had become tough and dependable.

Yamashita, known as Tiger of Malaya, was assigned to the Philippines to help General Homma in capitulating Bataan. Yamashita himself was under emotional stress. The son of a simple country doctor, he had not chosen the Army as a career in the beginning, but his father suggested the idea. He said, "Because I am big and healthy, and my mother did not object, because she believed, bless her soul, that I would never pass the highly competitive entrance examination." He was a heavyset man with bull neck and large head. He had an expressionless face and looked insensitive.

In March 10, General Wainwright was summoned to Corregidor where General Sutton informed him that MacArthur was leaving Corregidor the next evening by PT boat, which would take him and his family and staff to Mindanao, and from there they would board a Flying Fortress for Australia. He told Wainwright he would take command of all troops in the whole

Luzon area. He also asked Wainwright if he was agreeable to give General Jones another star and take over Wainwright's First Corps. Later, MacArthur came out of a small gray house at the eastern end of the Malinta Tunnel. He said to Wainwright, "I want you to make it known throughout all elements of your command that I'm leaving over my repeated protests." He had, however, considered disobeying direct orders from Washington so he could lead his troops to the end, but his advisers had persuaded him that he could do more in Australia for his beleaguered troops.

Wainwright said, "Of course, I will, Douglas."

"If I get to Australia, you know I'll come back as soon as I can with as much as I can."

"You will get through," replied Wainwright.

"And back." MacArthur gave Wainwright a box of cigars and two large jars of shaving cream. "Goodbye, Jonathan." They shook hands. "If you're still on Bataan when I get back, I'll make you a lieutenant general." The next evening, March 11 at about eight o'clock, a PT-41 boat commanded by Lieutenant John Bulkeley pulled out from Corregidor with General MacArthur; his wife; his four-year-old son, Arthur; General Sutherland; and several other officers. For thirty-five hectic hours, Lieutenant Bulkeley navigated his PT-41 through the enemy-controlled waters and, a little after dawn on March 13, made a landfall on the north coast of Mindanao, near the Del Monte pineapple factory. Before departing the PT-41, MacArthur told the commander that he would recommend him and the crew for the Silver Star. He continued, "You've taken me out of the jaws of death, and I won't forget it." On his arrival in Australia, MacArthur made a short note scribbled on a used envelope.

> The President of the United States ordered me to break through the Japanese lines and proceed from Corregidor to Australia for the purpose, as I understand it, of organizing the American offensive against Japan, a primary object of which is the relief of the Philippines. I came through and I shall return.

CHAPTER 8

The Fall Of Bataan

M aj. Gen. Edward King, Jr., Commander of the Luzon Force after Wainwright, was a modest man, courteous to all ranks, an artilleryman having wide experience in that field; he was an exemplary soldier, reasonable and realistic, and gave out orders in a quiet and undramatic way.

After the Japanese forces broke the line under the command of General Bluemel, he received a call from Wainwright giving him instructions to attack Homma's to cut in half. But King's troops were in the physical condition to attack. The Commander of First Philippine Corps, Maj. Gen. Albert M. Jones, thought any attack was senseless and told Wainwright directly he could not be persuaded. Wainwright told Jones to leave Major General King and hung up the phone. Major General Jones withdrew the lines in four phases and sent Brig. Gen. Arnold J. Funk to Corregidor to inform Wainwright that Bataan would be surrendering any minute.

Wainwright was very disturbed by the report from Brigadier General Funk. Wainwright was about to capitulate to the Japanese Forces. He would like to maintain their position as directed by MacArthur. Earlier, General MacArthur radioed General Wainwright, telling him that he was "utterly opposed under any circumstances or conditions to the ultimate capitulation of this command," and Wainwright should "prepare and execute an attack upon the enemy." Brigadier General Funk, with tears in his eyes said, "General, you know, of course, the situation over there. You know what the outcome will be." Wainwright replied, "I do."

Colonel Takeo ordered a huge flag of the rising sun hoist atop Mount Limay. Americans and Filipinos poured out of the jungles, fleeing from the advancing Japanese column. At the sea town of Mariveles, some boats were evacuating the fleeing soldiers to Corregidor. There was a mob and disorganized bunch of soldiers. Their attempt to cross did not materialize; the Japanese Navy patrol boat was on the lookout for the boats crossing the bay. Many boats sunk before they reached Corregidor.

Meanwhile, on April 8 at eleven thirty in the evening in Malinta Tunnel, General Wainwright phoned King to attack with Jones's First Corp. King relayed the orders to Jones who replied, "Any attack is ridiculous, out of the question." King agreed and said "Forget the attack" because he knew very well the condition of the Jones's First Corp. That same day at midnight, King summoned his staff and operation officer. He informed them that the situation was hopeless; there was no debate. Wainwright was now between two hard rocks MacArthur's explicit order to attack until the end and the soldier's unwillingness to fight.

While at this time, King took the burden upon his shoulder. He knew fully well that not carrying out orders would cause him to be court-martialed if he ever got back to the United States. But he weighed the balance between the seventy-eight thousand soldiers and his honor. He said, "I have decided to surrender Bataan." He did not communicate with Wainwright to keep him out of the picture or any part of the responsibility. Wainwright, upon learning of the surrender of General King, was upset and said, "Tell him not to do it." Later Wainwright regained his control. He radioed MacArthur.

> At 6 o'clock this morning General King . . . without my knowledge or approval sent a flag of truce to the Japanese commander. The minute I heard of it I disapproved of his action and directed that there would be no surrender. I was informed it was too late to make any change, that the action had already been taken.

That morning, General King, dressed in a clean set of uniform, went out to meet the Japanese officer who escorted him to place an Experimental Farm Station at Lamao. As he was on his way to meet the Japanese Commander, he was reminded of the history on Civil War when General Lee surrendered to General Grant at Appomattox on that same day, ninth of April. "Then there is nothing left to do but to go and see General Grant, and I would rather die a thousand deaths."

Soon a shiny black Cadillac drove up with Colonel Motoo Nakayama. Interpreter Colonel Nakayama, Homma's senior operation officer, asked King, "Are you General Wainwright?"

"No, I am General King, commander of all forces on Bataan." Nakayama was surprised and told him to get Wainwright and said the Japanese could not accept surrender without him. King said, "I could not communicate with Wainwright. My forces are no longer fighting units. I want to stop further bloodshed."

Colonel Nakayama said, "Surrender must be unconditional."

General King asked, "Will our troops be well treated?"

Colonel Nakayama replied, "We are not barbarians. Will surrender unconditionally?"

King sadly nodded. He had left his sword in Manila, so he presented his pistol instead and placed it on the table as a symbol of surrender.

American and Filipino soldiers huddled in a disconsolate bunch. There were tears of humiliation; however, some wept from the relief of knowing that at least their ordeal was over.

One U.S. Army Air Corps Captain Mark Wohlfeld saw some Japanese soldiers packing a mountain gun. They had big smiles on their faces and spoke gently. He said to himself that they were not bad after all. However, next came the Japanese infantry. Grim-faced, they began stripping the prisoners of blankets, watches, jewelry, razor blades, and even combs and toothbrushes. One Japanese soldier found from Wohlfeld some twenty rounds of .45 caliber ammunition and shouted to his comrade then beat him with his rifle butt.

And another saw the wedding ring on Lt. Col. Jack Sewell's finger and tried to yank it, but it could not be removed. The Japanese drew his bayonet and then approached Sewell. Sewell tried to remove it; he spat on his finger, but his mouth was too dry. He then rubbed his blood on his finger and finally was able to remove the ring and gave it to the Japanese soldier.

Japanese soldier on guard with fix bayonet.

CHAPTER 9

The Bataan Death March

On Bataan, the atrocious Death March began. About seventy thousand Filipino and American men began the march from Bataan to Camp O'Donnell, 144 kilometers away. Out of seventy thousand men, only fifty-four thousand completed the trip.

Virtually, ten thousand men died at the hands of the heartless Japanese on the Death March. Another six thousand managed to run away along the way. They marched all the way from Orion to Pilar to Abucay and to San Fernando, Pampanga. On their way, they kept their distance from the guards. Chances were, a prisoner could be hit by their rifle butts for no apparent reason at all.

They marched in fours, side by side in segmented columns, as many as a hundred men. Usually, trouble came to those who were at the side or perimeter of the column because they were directly exposed to the Japanese guards. Every time a prisoner dropped off the middle ranks, it became a challenge on who could occupy the vacant space to avoid close contact with the guards. A marcher's position could mean life or death.

On one occasion, one prisoner was swaying out of the line. A Japanese tank driver deliberately swerved his tank, ran over the staggering prisoner, and the other tanks followed suit. The soldier's body, like a corrugated galvanized iron sheet, was flattened—guts and blood sprawling and eyes coming out of the sockets, rolling on the hot asphalt road. Some who got weak stomach, threw up at the sight of the run-down body. If they broke the line, the guards, with their bayonets, would surely stab them not deep enough to make them suffer from pain.

The soldiers were so thirsty; some took the chance of drinking water from the carabao (water buffalo) mudhole. The Japanese had no pity on them, and they even bayoneted them to death.

An American POW receiving medical treatment
from Japanese Medic

MAP OF EVACUATION ROUTE

Advancing Japanese troops in Bataan.

American and Filipino troops marching across Bataan
(Bataan Death March)

American soldiers surrenders.

American and Filipino troops in line formation receiving
instructions from the Japanese soldier.

Japanese Landing forces carrying their provisions.

Japanese soldiers entering the coconut plantation.

Japanese guards pushing back the prisoners.

Japanese guard watching prisoners taking a short break.

The Death March

Prisoners of war exhausted from heat and thirst while Japanese
soldier with fix bayonet keep an eye.

Japanese soldier stand guard on pow resting after long march.

Camp O'Donnel concentration camp

Filipinos, being devoted Catholics and Christians, saw this scene like a tragic passage reminiscent of Christ suffering on His way toward Golgotha. Women openly wept and bravely gave food and water to the starving prisoners. Some were killed for giving food or water. They braved and lined up even in the face of death. Sometimes, the Japanese would allow the prisoners to accept the food; many times, they would not let the prisoners accept.

The Japanese could not swallow what they saw. They saw Filipinos demonstrating their overwhelming support to the United States by fighting and dying alongside the Americans. They could not understand why the Filipinos, their fellow Asians, gave their lives to support the Americans when they, the Japanese, Asians like them, were not honored and respected.

After the death march had passed through, the roads were in indescribable shamble of mixed human flesh and their belongings—canteen, towels, mess kits, hats, shoes, shirts, fess, urine, blood, guts, and smashed up dead bodies and flies all over them. The townspeople picked up the bodies and buried them on the roadside. Some civilians with bayonet-stabbed wounds lay dead by the roadside. There was a decapitated body with the head attached to it only by a thread of their uncut veins.

On the other hand, the Japanese government in Tokyo expected that they would soon occupy the Philippines and would give them wide amnesty and show benevolence at every possible turn. General Masaharu Homma, the commanding general of the entire Japanese invading forces, for one, espoused a policy of mercy toward the Filipinos; however, a certain Colonel Masanobu Tsuji, a member of the high command, was totally against the mercy policy. Instead, he advocated seizing total control of the people through act of terror and immediate retribution to those showing friendship toward the United States.

As witnessed by one survivor of the concentration camp, on their way to Camp O'Donnell as they were marching through the barrio, a barefooted, pregnant young woman, with her sympathetic eyes pooled with tears, came to offer food to the prisoners. The Japanese guards dragged her by her hair and took her by a tree and forced her and later bayoneted her and gouged out her fetus.

A story as witnessed by Mr. Dominador Noche, during the famous Bataan Death March, he was one of the captured soldiers. He was private first class in the Philippine Army in the Medical Corps assigned to the Fiftieth Regular Division under General Segundo. As they were forced to march toward Camp O'Donnell from Orion, Bataan, the heat was unbearable.

He was so thirsty that when they were given a break, he lay down on some grass and tried to feel the cool dew from the grass. At one time, he saw that a fellow prisoner had a soda bottle of water; he begged for water. The fellow prisoner said that he could not give it since it did not belong to him; it belonged to another prisoner who happened to be his friend. He asked his friend for the water; it was given to him, and he drank half of the bottle. While they were walking, one of the prisoners had quit walking. His fellow prisoners tried to help him up, but he refused. A Japanese guard tried to help, but the prisoner would not stand. Another Japanese guard on a bicycle came by and assisted to raise the prisoner. Again, the prisoner would not stand, and the marching came to a sudden stop. The guard with the bicycle grabbed his rifle and struck the prisoner with his bayonet and ordered the other prisoners to take the body on a nearby sugar plantation. After arriving at Camp O'Donnell, they boarded a train in a boxcar. At first, the door was left open; but Filipino civilians, seeing the prisoners starving, threw at the open door any kind of food they could gather. The Japanese guards closed the door, which made the boxcar hotter; sweat and vomits and shit and all were all over the boxcar. The boxcar smelled so terrible that a healthy person could get sick or would throw up.

In several instance, some soldiers could no longer walk; the others gave them a helping hand, and when the guard saw this, the guard pulled out the weakling and bayoneted him because the weakling was dragging the rest of the marchers. Some prisoners were so sick with dysentery that they had to defecate every now and then. They could not stop, so they just shit and peed in their pants. When they arrived in San Fernando, they were herded in the cattle boxcar with no window and was a standing room only. The heat was unbearable.

The foul smell of the body shit and pee and the heat were beyond what any person or even animal could take. Some of the prisoners were so sick they threw out, vomited, and the foul air made the others get sick too. As one Filipino soldier related his experience during the Death March, he was forced to march with hundreds of Filipino and American suffering men; he had seen the outrageous brutality and the ease with which the Japanese guards ignored the cries of the wounded. He began to feel a low, burning sensation, something stirring, rising up to his brain from a dark hidden place. He had drawn from the eyes of his captors, who treated their prisoners with vicious disregard. On the long brutal march, the Japanese guards had ignored the desperate and dying, the men who begged for water. He was so tired and thirsty. He walked staggering, trying his best to stand erect, but his legs were too weak to support his body. The guards would use their bayonets to poke him. At one time, he had to stop, and he just sat in a squat position. The guards kicked him at the back, making him more unable to stand. The guard raised his rifle, and when he was about to strike him with the bayonet, he rolled to his side, and the sharp steel barely missed him. Another guard came over and stopped the other guards who were about to strike him again.

Another Japanese enlisted man stole a ring just as his commanding officer passed by. The officer noticed the ring bore the University of Notre Dame insignia. He hit the looter in the face and returned the ring to its owner. He asked the owner of the ring, "When did you graduate?"

The officer replied, "In 1935."

Several steps away, the Japanese officer looked back and said, "I graduated from Southern California in '35."

CHAPTER 10

Corregidor Surrenders

Wainwright's intolerable burden was somewhat lightened by a message from Roosevelt.

> *I am keenly aware of the tremendous difficulties under which you are waging your great battle. The physical exhaustion of your troops obviously precludes the possibility of a major counterattack unless our efforts to rush food to you should prove successful. Because of the state [over] which your forces have no control, I am modifying my orders to you . . . my purpose is to leave to your best judgment any decision affecting the future of Bataan garrison . . . I feel it proper and necessary that you should assured of complete freedom of action and of my will of confidence in the wisdom of whatever decision you may be forced to make.*

On April 29, the day of birth of Emperor Hirohito was celebrated by the Japanese artillery; fire and bombing reached a climax. Ammunition damps exploded, solid rocks disintegrated, and grass fires swept the island. Then bombardment concentrated on the big mortars of Batteries.

On the following day, sixteen thousand shells bursted on the island. The beach defenders just crouched in the shallow foxholes, filled with hatred to those in the safety hold in the tunnel. In May 3, General Wainwright sent a message to MacArthur: "SITUATION HERE IS PAST BECOMING DESPERATE." He also wrote a letter to General Marshall.

> IN MY OPINION THE ENEMY IS CAPABLE OF MAKING ASSAULT ON CORREGIDOR AT ANY TIME. SUCCESS OR FAILURE OF SUCH ASSAULT WILL DEPEND ENTIRELY ON THE STEADFASTNESS OF BEACH DEFENSE TROOPS. CONSIDERING THE PRESENT LEVEL OF MORALE, I ESTIMATE THAT WE HAVE SOMETHING LESS THAN AN EVEN CHANCE TO BEAT OFF AN ASSAULT. I HAVE GIVEN YOU, IN ACCORDANCE WITH YOUR REQUEST, A VERY FRANK AND HONEST OPINION ON THE SITUATION AS I SEE IT.

When the Japanese landed in Corregidor on May 5, Wainwright knew it was over. The next day May 6, he reluctantly sent a message to President Roosevelt.

Later, General Jonathan Wainwright, representing the U.S. Forces and the Philippine Army, surrendered to Lt. Gen. Masaharu Homma, commanding general of the Japanese Imperial Armed Forces in Southeast Asia.

Finally, the guns in Corregidor had silenced. General Jonathan Wainwright sent his last radiogram to President Roosevelt.

> *With broken heart and head bowed in sadness but not in shame I report to your excellency that today I must arrange terms for the surrender of the fortified island of Manila Bay . . . there is a limit of human endurance and that limit has long since been passed. Without prospect of relief I feel it is my duty to my country and to my gallant troops to end the useless effusion of blood and human sacrifice. If you agree Mr. President, please say to the nation that my troops and I have accomplished all that is humanly possible and that we have upheld the best traditions of the United States and its army. May god bless and preserve you and guide you and the nation in the effort to ultimate victory . . . with profound regret and with continued pride in my gallant troops I go to meet the Japanese commander. Goodbye, Mr. President.*

All American guns ceased firing. General Wainwright went to his Chevrolet car and waited for two hours and told the driver to drive east, passing the Denver Hill. He continued on foot and passed through several Filipino and American soldiers' bodies lying around. They were later approached by an arrogant young Japanese lieutenant who said that surrender must include all American and Filipino troops in the island. General Wainwright said, "I do not choose to discuss surrender terms with you. Take me to your senior officer." Colonel Motoo Nakayama, who accepted the surrender of General King, stepped forward.

Wainwright told him, "I would surrender the four islands in Manila Bay." Colonel Motoo Nakayama said that General Homma instructed him to take General Wainwright to Bataan for surrender ceremonies. At that time, the General did not expect that Wainwright was surrendering because the night before, twenty-one landing boats were sunk, and the landing did not fully materialize. Upon hearing of Wainwright's intention to surrender, Homma was very much relieved because of the heavy pressure from Tokyo for a long time for the capitulation of the Philippines. At four o'clock in the afternoon, Wainwright—leaning heavily on his cane, body thin and bent—again stepped on Bataan soil at Cabcaben. Two cars brought him to a blue house surrounded by mango grove. The Americans waited for General Homma on the open porch. From there, they could see Manila in the south and could see Corregidor still burning, erupting, shell bursting. As far as the Japanese were concerned, the war in the Philippines had not yet ended because the Southern Visayas was still not occupied. Finally, a black Cadillac drew up and a barrel-chested General Homma, looking crisp and vigorous in his olive drab uniform, stepped out. He welcomed the Americans. "You must be very tired and weary." General Wainwright thanked him and all in the porch, and then handed his signed surrender papers surrendering the four islands. General Homma was disappointed at the surrender terms. Homma would like to have all the Philippines surrendered, but General Wainwright said that the southern Philippines was not under his command, but he had authority over General Sharp to surrender the southern Philippines. The southern Philippines was under the command of General Sharp. General Homma said to his new chief of staff, "What shall we do, Wachi?" Major General Wachi said, "I feel General Wainwright is lying." The general then said, "Send them back to Corregidor, and in case we cannot continue the negotiation, let us continue the battle. Go back to Corregidor and think it over. I called the meeting over, Good day." He nodded and returned to his Cadillac. General Wainwright and his party left Bataan and returned to

Corregidor. General Wainwright was now placed between two hard rocks. They were accompanied by Nakayama. Wainwright asked, "What shall we do now?"

Nakayama said, "We will take you and your party back to Corregidor, and you can do what you damn please." The entire failed negotiation was done through an interpreter, even if General Homma understood the English language very well. This was done because of the other Japanese present. The only other person who knew what was really going on was a bilingual newspaperman named Kazumaro Uno who had been raised in Utah. He sympathized with the plight of the Americans and explained to Nakayama that Wainwright was ready to surrender all the Philippines. Nakayama, somewhat mollified, said to Wainwright that he would accompany him to Corregidor and added, "First thing tomorrow morning, you will go to Homma with a new surrender term and promise to contact the other forces in the Philippines." Colonel Traywick was empowered to arrest General Sharp if he disobeyed the orders from General Wainwright to surrender. Wainwright said to Colonel Traywick, "Jesse, I'm depending on you to carry out these orders." General Wainwright and five of his staff officers were taken by assault boat to Lamao. At Lamao, they waited for two hours; they were given some food—rice and bony fish. At about eleven o'clock, Lieutenant Hisamichi Kano of the Propaganda Corps, who had been educated in New York and New Jersey, greeted Wainwright and offered the Americans some fruit. Wainwright was having problem reading the prepared message, and Kano rewrote the message to colloquial English. A Filipino radio announcer, Marcel Victor Young, was on hand.

Shortly before midnight, General Wainwright, sitting on a bamboo stool with a microphone on small bamboo table, read his message to all forces in the Philippines. He directed General Sharp to surrender his troops in the southern forces. He choked several times while reading his message. It was very difficult for him to deliver the message of capitulation. Marcel Victor Young signed off at 12:20 AM, May 8. Kano then led the emotionally drained General and his staff to the next room and gave him some drinks from a Scotch bottle. The speech was heard by Filipino and American soldiers. General Sharp could not believe what he just heard. He sent a radio message to General MacArthur. MacArthur replied to Sharp.

Orders emanating from General Wainwright have no validity. If possible separate your force into small elements and initiate guerilla operations. You, of course, have full authority to make any decision

> *that immediate emergency may demand. Keep in communication with me as much as possible. You are a gallant and resourceful commander and I am proud of what you have done.*

Two days later, Colonel Traywick arrived to see General Sharp. Sharp read the letter from General Wainwright, and after reading, he concluded that there was no other alternative but to go along with General Wainwright's orders. At once he radioed General MacArthur, "DIRE NECESSITY ALONE HAS PROMPTED THIS ACTION." General MacArthur sent a radio message to General Marshall.

> *I have just received word from Major General Sharp that General Wainwright in two broadcast of the night of 7/8 announced he was reassuming command of all forces in the Philippines and directed their surrender giving in detail the method of accomplishment. I believe Wainwright has temporarily become unbalanced and his condition renders him susceptible of enemy use.*

After the surrender, Homma had forbidden pillage and rape and ordered his troops not to regard the Filipinos as enemies but to respect their custom, traditions, and religion.

General Count Hisaichi Terauchi, commander of the Southern Army, was displeased with Homma's lenient treatment of Filipino civilians. Homma told Terauchi that the Americans never did exploit the Philippines. "They administered a very benevolent supervision over the Philippines. Japan should establish an even better and more enlightened supervision." General Count Terauchi was influenced by Colonel Tsuji to retaliate secretly. Using Homma's name, they sent out orders countermanding his liberal policy. Homma was unaware of the capture of Chief Justice Jose Abad Santos in Negros province who was later transferred to Cebu and executed under his order. Maj. Gen. Kiyotake Kawaguchi, commander of the Visayan Japanese forces, bursted into General Homma, accusing him of the execution of Jose Abad Santos, which was against Homma's order. He said, "This was outrageous betrayal of Bushido and the Emperor." Kawaguchi had thrown out a staff officer, Inuzuka, who insisted on the execution of Chief Justice Jose Abad Santos and his son as well. Two weeks later, Kawaguchi received an order to send the two Santoses to Mindanao for immediate execution. Kawaguchi was so angry that he crumpled up the message. Kawaguchi summoned the father and son and told them he had done his utmost to save their lives but now was forced to execute the elder Santos in the name of the Fourteenth Army. "I promised to protect your son, so don't worry," he told the father. Santos said he had never been anti-Japanese. "I appreciate your kindness toward me and my son and wish glory for your country." He said to his son, "When you see your mother, give my love. I will soon die. Be a man of honor and work for the Philippines." Santos was taken to the nearby coconut tree and bound and blindfolded. He made his cross and was shot by a firing squad.

Field Marshal Count Hisaichi Terauchi

Kawaguchi reported to General Homma about the execution of Chief Justice Santos. Homma, upon hearing it, was dumbfounded. He too had high regard for Chief Justice Santos. He remembered his approval for clemency of Santos's execution requested by Kawaguchi. He told Kawaguchi, "I regret very much what had happened." The following day, Kawaguchi confronted Hayashi. "What a *keshikaran* [shameful] thing you did!" he burst out. "I trusted you as my classmate." Hayashi was defensive. Homma had already admonished him, "But." He excused himself. "Imperial Headquarters was so insistent about the execution of Santos." "Who do you mean by Imperial Headquarter?" "It was Tsuji."

Several weeks later, General Manuel Roxas, a former Speaker of the House, was captured in Mindanao. A message coming from Manila ordered General Torao Ikuta to execute General Manuel Roxas "secretly and immediately."

The order was authorized in the name of Homma and stamped by Hayashi and three staff officers. General Ikuta in Bataan had refused to shoot prisoners without written order. He found himself incapable to act and turned over this responsibility to Colonel Nobuhiko Jimbo, a balding man with glasses and a mustache like that of Tojo. Being a Catholic, Jimbo was tormented while he drove Roxas and the Governor to the execution place, which took them more than an hour. The Governor was begging for his life, saying that he was not a soldier like Roxas, and kept on begging Jimbo. His voice became hysterical that Roxas tried to calm him down and said, "Look at the *sampaguita*." He pointed at clusters of delicate white blossoms, the national flower of the Philippines. "Aren't they beautiful?" Jimbo, thinking of the samurai Bushido code, (no samurai could have acted more nobly) decided to try to save Roxas no matter what the consequences. He left his two prisoners under guard in a small town and returned to Davao; somehow, he had persuaded General Ikuta to ignore the execution order. They could not keep the secret for long. An officer arrived from Manila. Jimbo was to be court-martialed for his high-handed action. Jimbo flew to Manila to meet General Homma, but Homma was not available at the time. He spoke with General Wachi. After hearing this, Wachi could not believe such an order had gone out, particularly after Homma's violent reaction to the execution of Santos. Jimbo showed him the order. However, General Wachi could not cancel the orders with General Homma's stamp. He made an order countermanding the original order that suspended the execution. He told Jimbo to wait inside, and he burst out the door to Hayashi's office and confronted Hayashi. "Who gave this order of execution?" Hayashi and the three staff officer denied. Jimbo, hearing this from the other room, went in and showed the document to the three with their names on it. They were forced to confess. There was a pause, and Hayashi shouted at Jimbo, "You have done a terrible thing to us." Wachi told Jimbo that Homma was very pleased with his action. So Roxas was saved. After the war, General Roxas was elected president of the Philippines.

CHAPTER 11

The Compassionate Poet General

Lt. Gen. Masaharu Homma, a son of a landowner, was one of the best warriors of Japan during the Second World War. He was enormously relieved that Bataan had fallen. However, he does not feel victorious at all because he had not obtained what he sought to accomplish—the surrender of Corregidor. He was having a very serious complication between the transportation of Filipino-American soldiers and Corregidor. Tokyo insisted that he should capture Corregidor soon so that the shipping lane passing through Corregidor would be safe for maritime transportation. General Homma, as a well-concerned person who had a wide experience of many countries he visited including the United States, was concerned about the treatment of the prisoners of war. General Homma had foreseen the enormous evacuation problem a month earlier and had commissioned some of his best officers to address the problem. The officers presented their ideas to General Homma. On paper, they appeared decent and humane. They incarcerated the prisoners in Camp O'Donnell in the northeast of the Bataan peninsula. The route would be passing several towns—Cabcaben, Lamao, Limay, Orion, Pilar, Balanga, Orani, Lubao and, finally, San Fernando, where they would take a train ride to Capas, which was very near to the station. Those who could walk would walk no more than ten kilometers a day. Food and shelter would be provided. For those who were sick, transportation would be provided. Two field hospitals capable of treating one thousand patients would be set up. He had two plans for the transportation of prisoners of war. Both plans failed because first, his officers grossly underestimated the number of prisoners of war. Their projected estimate was that twenty-five thousand Filipino and American troops would surrender. The actual number was one hundred thousand. Homma even ordered his planners to go back and estimate again. The new estimate was forty thousand. Homma was pleased with the estimate, not knowing it was short of sixty thousand men. At the same time, he was preoccupied in the planning of his strategy against Corregidor. It was important to Homma that the prisoners of war be treated fairly. Homma instructed his officers to treat the Filipino and American captives "with a friendly spirit" in accordance with the Geneva Convention. Homma was aware that the Emperor himself had instructed Japanese soldiers to view foreign POWs as "unfortunate individuals" and to handle them with "utmost benevolence and kindness." During the Japanese-Russo War, the prisoners of war were treated humanely. As per their standard Army instruction that had been written in 1904, it had plainly outlined a policy of mercy. "A Prisoner of War," it said, "shall be treated with spirit of goodwill and shall never be subjected to cruelties or humiliation." Homma took this said instruction by heart.

Homma was good-looking, about six feet two inches in height, and well-mannered. Because of his height, he looked like a giant among the many Japanese during that era. He divorced his wife after learning she became a prostitute. He was somewhat idiosyncratic aesthete, unhappily trapped inside the confines of Bushido discipline. He liked to paint and compose poetry. It was ironic that he was assigned to attack the Philippines; he was democratic-minded and openly pro-Western. He spoke fluent English, traveled in America, and loved American movies. In 1938, he traveled in Nanking and authored a book about the Japanese atrocities that had occurred during the Japanese occupation. In April 9, thousands of Americans and Filipinos stumbled out of the jungles, sucking sugar cane stalk and waving white towels and bedsheets. Homma had great confidence in his Fourteenth Army evacuation plan. He even told one American officer, "Your worries are now over. Japan treats their prisoners well. You may see my country in cherry blossom time. That is a beautiful sight."

The desecration of American Flag.

Japanese soldiers yelling "Banzai".

Taken in Corregidor Island after Japanese captured the island.

CHAPTER 12

The Fall of the Philippines

The ceremony was in Corregidor Island. The thirteen thousand survivors in Corregidor surrendered on May 6, 1942. Before his departure for United States, President Manuel L. Quezon advised Dr. Jose P. Laurel to stay behind and cooperate in the civil administration of the Japanese occupation. President Quezon also appointed Jorge B. Vargas as mayor of the city of Manila. Vargas had the duty to hand over the city to the Japanese conquerors. President Quezon hoped that his advice would make the occupation less severe. Some of the Philippine elite followed Laurel's moral example. Others collaborated extensively with the Japanese occupation forces. During the occupation, Vargas was chairman of the Philippine Executive Commission. Vargas appointed Leon G. Guinto as the mayor of Manila City. Many despised President Laurel and his wartime government. After the arrival of the invading forces, there was no government to represent the people of the Philippines. Dr. Jose P. Laurel then took the initiative and responsibility to represent the people of the Philippines, and General Mateo Capinpin was appointed to head the Philippine Constabulary. The rest of the Filipinos and Americans who did not surrender or who escaped from the Death March, made their way to the mountain and established the guerrilla movement. The organization of the guerrilla units cannot be justly attributed to a single man or group of men. Rather, it was more the inevitable results of the Japanese policy of hurrying up Japanizing the Philippines. This fatal policy of the Japanese and the equally grievous corollary of literally beating the not-too-eager people into wholehearted cooperation did not accomplish the expected. Thus, it did not take long before the people defied enemy occupation and control. Many of these people, who first bore arms against the Japanese after the fall, were unsurrendered soldiers. Many others were civilians who, for purely patriotic or personal reasons, took it upon themselves to defy the enemy. At the outskirt, however, and in some places, condition brought about by this flare-up of renewed resistance resulted in chaos. Gradually, however, the more stable minds began to assert themselves, and toward the period of July—August of 1942, things began to take shape on the formation of military groups under recognized leaders. In the Visayan Islands, conflict arose between several leaders. Peralta claimed the whole Visayan Islands but later settled in Panay. Mata (one of our neighbors in Camp Murphy before the outbreak of the war) had his own unit in Negros, one of the most powerful groups. Ausejo's and Mercado's units included a so-called Puring Group, which was led by two brothers—one was a private first class and the other was an ex-convict who believed that since they were the ones who voluntarily banded together to fight the enemy, no one had the right to butt in and infringe their independent rights. Abcede aligned with Peralta. In Cebu were Fenton and Cushing who until Fenton began to get scandalously involved with women that his popularity began to decrease. This started in February. Cushing's popularity, on the other hand, was somewhat dimmed by Fenton's due to the latter's more intimate knowledge of bombast and ballyhoo, which was regarded by people to be a much better leader.

In Luzon, greater confusion reigned between guerrilla leaders. Most guerrillas were scattered in groups without the benefit of able leadership. The largest ones were headed by a former bus driver named Marcos Villa Agustin who was known as Marking his unit. This unit was reported to have indiscriminately enlisted thousands of members and issued commission up to the rank of colonel. One famous name at the time was Yay Panlilio, former photo reporter of DMHM, Intelligence Agent of the United States Army, Badge number 67 in Fort William McKinley. Another unit in existence in Luzon was that of Col. E. P. Jones, which called itself the American-Filipino Forces in the Far East, Philippine Fourth Army Corps, East Central Luzon Guerrilla Area. There were various other units including those of Nakar, Vinzons, and of Governor Escudero and Major Lapuz. Both of them operated in Sorsogon. There was also the HUKBALAHAP, short for the Tagalog *Hukbo ng Bayan Laban sa mga Hapon,* an army against Japanese under Professor Lava, formerly of the University of the Philippines. This organization was supposedly composed of Communists from Pampanga. In Cebu, trouble between Fenton and Cushing, who had actually been operating satisfactorily during the early days of the guerrilla, began to manifest itself until it got so complicated that an open outbreak finally resulted, beginning with Cushing's travel to the headquarters against Fenton's wish and ending in Fenton's arrest, trial, and execution by his own officers and men. In Leyte, Kangleon and Miranda (my former ROTC Commandant) had their own troubles, which had reached the status of civil war. In Mindoro, there was a dispute between Beloncio and Ruffy; this resulted in the split of the faction. Jurado, a U.S. Naval Academy graduate, was sent to patch up the difference but was slain by the two opposing guerrilla units. My father, who was inducted in USAFFE (United States Army Forces Far East) as Captain in Chemical Warfare, surrendered to the Japanese as ordered by the high command. After his release from the concentration camp in Capas, he attempted to join the guerrilla movement several times but was turned down because of his surrender to the Japanese. Upon hearing about the conflict between Beloncio and Ruffy and which caused the death of Jurado, my father backed out and decided to wait until the liberation of the Philippines. He said, "Filipinos are fighting each other. That is wrong. They should fight the enemy instead." He, however, provided military intelligence to the guerrilla to be transmitted to the higher echelon.

Japanes reconizant patrol searching for guerillas

85

CHAPTER 13

Return To Manila From Pagsanjan

We arrived in Manila by a cattle truck. We returned to our apartment. I was very curious of the Japanese soldiers. I watched several tanks rumbling on the main street. As they moved along, there were soldiers walking beside and behind the tanks. Their faces looked grim and battle-hardened, probably because of combat fatigue. No friendly faces, they looked very stern and hardened. Some Filipinos and Japanese civilians waved the Japanese flag as if they were welcoming them to the city. We just stayed behind closed windows and doors. We peeked through the broken *kapis* pane.

Had we stayed in Manila, we would have surely starved to death, Mom thought. She therefore decided to move out of the apartment secretly. That evening with the help of Usting Root, they dug a deep hole and buried all my father's military paraphernalia. On the following morning, she informed the property owner that we would be back soon to settle the back account. We would go to her relative in Kawit. Mom made her escape plans; one of Mom's greatest challenge was how she could move her family of eight whose ages ranged from six months to ten years old. Our youngest then was Ligaya-Carmen, "Baby," and the oldest was me. Mom had to find a way that she could move us out of the city without being detected by the occupation troops. With the help of Tia Tibang (her elder sister) and two house helpers, we were able to sneak out of the city. We made it just in time before the Japanese authorities issued an order on travel restrictions. The Japanese placed roadblocks and sentries on all exits and entrances to Manila. These sentries had strict orders to check all people from age ten and above to show an identity card or passes issued by the Japanese occupation government. These identity cards and passes must be surrendered to them upon demand by the sentry guard.

CHAPTER 14

Escape to Mindoro

We escaped to Mindoro, stopping over in Cabuyao about thirty miles south of Manila and then in Binakayan, Kawit, Cavite, the birthplace of my mother. Here we stayed in Impong Tayo's farm for a week. He was a distant relative. In his yard were many *atis* and *chico* fruit trees. After a brief stay, Mom hired a cattle truck driver to take us to Lemery, Batangas. We traveled by a circuitous route via Tagaytay Ridge. Two of my sisters and us five brothers were seated in the open cargo flat with Tia Tibang and our two helpers, Usting Root and Teresita, and Mom with Baby (Ligaya-Carmen) seated in the front cab with the driver.

We left Binakayan, Kawit, in early evening; we traveled by night to avoid detection by Japanese troopers. Along the winding rough and rugged road, which had been recently paved, with no asphalt or road barrier on the side, we traveled. On our right was a steep rocky mountainside, and on our left was a deep ravine. As we slowly drove through this winding rough and rugged road, as we looked down the deep ravine in a far distant, with the fog blanketing the side of the mountain, we saw the beautiful islet of Taal Volcano, a volcano within a volcano in the middle of Taal Lake. The trip was very hazardous. On several occasions, while our truck would maneuver around the sharp curve where to back off was necessary, the truck's rear tire would hang precariously off the cliff. After several attempts, we would proceed, beset by a Japanese sentry. As we approached the sentry, it was slightly foggy; the mountain breeze chilled us; we did not have any blanket. It was so cold; I could not keep my teeth from chattering.

CHAPTER 15

Our First Encounter with a Japanese Soldier

We were searched by a guard for contrabands, which was our first Japanese encounter. As we were approaching the Japanese Sentry, the guard waved the driver to stop. His uniform was very much different from those I have seen in my early days. His headgear looked like a khaki baseball cap with five pointed stars in front and strips of white cloth attached at the back of the cap. They appeared to me like a small curtain, I guessed to protect the back of their neck from the heat of the sun. He wore a khaki jacket with white shirt inside and khaki pants. From the knee down to his ankle was a band legging, and his *tabi* shoes had split toes. On his hand was a *numbu* rifle with fixed bayonet. The sentry guard spoke broken English.

He shouted, "*Kurrah, Kurrah.*"

And he motioned us to disembark from the truck and pointed his finger to the roadside. The Japanese went up the truck and started inspecting our belongings; he opened all suitcases, searching for contrabands. While the soldier was opening and digging our belongings, Mom, who was sitting in front, was busy praying for help. She was chanting with her rosary on her hands. She remembered the picture of my father in military uniform and a set of travel orders placed between layers of clothing, which she herself packed a week ago before our retreat from the city. Inside the suitcase was a crucifix of Jesus Christ. The Japanese made a diligent search on and about those suitcases but found nothing except our clothes. It was a miracle. Had

89

the Japanese found those picture and papers, we would have been detained and probably questioned and delayed in our travel. The Japanese soldier, having found nothing of importance to him, told us to embark.

The soldier then inquired Mom, "Omae dare des' ka?" Who are you?

Mom, smiling and pointing to the driver, said, "Me his wife."

The Japanese soldier looked at us and said, "Ah, takusan kodomo san." Ah, lots of kids. We were shivering because the morning breeze was very cold coming from the mountain. He thought we were afraid of him. He then told us to embark and then told the driver to proceed. As we were moving out, the soldier who inspected us was reprimanded and chewed out by the sergeant of the guard.

The sergeant yelled at him, exclaiming, "Bakaya ero, bakkatare." Stupid, stupid fool.

He then slapped and kicked the soldier. I do not know for what reason he was chewed out. This may be an example of barbaric action by a superior officer, which were later reflected to the innocent civilians.

We arrived in Lemery, Batangas, that same morning. We went to Dad's cousins (the Inumerables of Taal) where we rested and refreshed ourselves for our next journey. A small cup of heavily brewed chocolate and salt bread was served to us to give us more energy. We waited for the signal to proceed to our destination—Mindoro. Uncle Macario (Dad's cousin) chartered a sailboat that would take us to Mindoro. We waited until dark, took a calesa—a horse-pulled cart—that took us to the beach, and secretly boarded the sailboat under cover of darkness. Mom hired a boat *batil* (a single-masted wooden sailboat about thirty feet high and fifteen feet wide). Inside the sailboat was a big space, nothing but an empty hold. Mom and my younger siblings stayed inside the *camarote* (cabin). We sailed out to the sea under cover of darkness to conceal ourselves from the ever-persisting Japanese Navy Patrol Boats. The Japanese Navy operated routine patrol to stop stragglers going to Mindoro because Mindoro Island was considered a hostile area. Every now and then, we would hear the approaching danger and watch the red and green running lights of the patrol boat fast approaching us; our elders seemed to be so tense and feared the possibility of being detected by the patrol. We, the kids, were not so much aware about the danger we were facing. Luck was with us; the patrol boat changed course before they got close to us. The sky was clear and full of stars but no moon. It was so silent; we heard nothing except the slapping of water against the hull of the sailboat and the slicing sound of the smooth water as the boat cut through it. I listened to the very pleasing sound of the bubbles from the wake.

Our travel was over a smooth, fair wind and following sea. There was no disturbing sound except the squeaking sound of the rattan vine fastened around the mast and lanyard and of the wind slapping against the sail as it swung from port to starboard side of the boat. A few hours later, we passed through a channel between Isla Verde and Batangas; we saw several flickering lights from the houses on the seashore. We traded sailing to take advantage of the prevailing wind and to keep us away from the Japanese Patrol Boats. The Japanese Navy Patrol Boats were on the lookout for sailboats going to Mindoro; they had ordered to sink any sailboat sighted. Luckily, none of us suffered from seasickness. Several times I stepped onto the main deck to enjoy the breeze and the sight of disappearing island in the horizon. At this time, my mom was busy thinking of where she was going to get our provision for the coming days, weeks, or months. She knew nothing of selling, gardening, or any sort of livelihood.

Nothing can happen. The Filipino way of thinking, *bahala na,* always comes in the agreeable situation. In the end, something will always come our way. I think it is always the divine assistance through the medium of prayer. Nothing is impossible. When at lost, some miraculous thing is always going to happen. It always happens, and it never misses. I can still see my mom's tired face, but it still has the love, care, and smile despite the hardship from the past months and the fast approaching unknown future. She was always a very positive person in all her endeavors—a very practical person who used her five senses and least used the non-sense. She thinks better of the solution to the problem when desperate situation occurs.

Japanese Sentry about to check our baggage

CHAPTER 16

The Strange Land

After a long hazardous trip, we finally dropped anchor on the beach of Malaylay, Baco, Mindoro. I was standing at the bow of the sailboat, nervous, not knowing what was ahead of us, looking at the panoramic view of a long sandy black beach lined with coconut trees and fishing boats beached on the shore. Looking farther away, I saw the great mountain, Mount Halcon, like a giant looming on at us. The word *Mindoro* is a Spanish word meaning "Mina de Oro," in English, "Mine of gold." Standing ashore eager to meet us was Inay Ilyang (my father's mother), wearing her typical Filipina *patajong,* which is sarong and *kimona,* and her *salakot,* a straw sun hat.

Not far from Malaylay, we then proceeded to Pambisan. As we approached, our new neighbors welcomed us. While my mom was busy talking with our neighbors, I was very curious of the surroundings, and the kids were shy. There were coconut trees everywhere I looked; there was no road, path, or trail, and many wild plants were growing around the houses. The houses were raised from the ground about five feet. I looked at the house where we were going to stay; it was a huge house, and it was made entirely of Philippine mahogany. The house was elevated about ten feet from the ground; the posts were visible, having about twelve inches in diameter. The stairs going to the floor was six feet wide and fifteen feet long, all made of *narra* wood. We stayed at this house, Lolo Martin's huge house. He was my mother's father.

Because of food shortage, we stayed there for a short time. Mom realized that should we stay in Pambisan, we would not last long due to food shortage, and our provisions were all exhausted. Mom then decided to go to Nagpatay (the interior country) even if it was against her will; she had no other choice but to go along with the suggestion of her mother-in-law. Having no husband to support her eight children, it became very difficult for her to be with her in-laws. However, with our few belongings, it was easy for us to pack our baggage. We moved to upstream Nagpatay. We boarded a *paraw*—a long narrow outrigger canoe. It was our first experience to ride such a boat. We paddled our way through the freshwater river. The river was so clean and clear; I can even see the white pebbles at the bottom of the river. Clean it was, but beware when drinking it; any person can catch malaria from the water. The current was so strong and cold because the water was coming from Mount Halcon. I had some flashbacks from the movies I had seen before the war, like *Tarzan the Ape Man* with Chita and Jane. We paddled through a very wide freshwater river. From a distance, we heard birds singing, monkeys crying and saw crocodiles sunbathing and yawning lazily on the riverbanks and iguanas on treetops, eating and chewing buds. It was so exciting to see a real wildlife. We were all experiencing a culture shock. The people around us did not understand why we felt that way.

We arrived in Nagpatay, a place way out in the boondocks. The riverbank was so steep; they built stairs of clay and rocks. As soon as we reached the top of the bank, there stood a nipa hut, our temporary home. The house was a small bamboo-stilt hut. The roof and sidings of which were made of nipa palm leaves stringed together by rattan strips using bamboo stake for stiffener. The flooring was made of bamboo stakes; even the stairs were made of bamboo poles split in half. Not a single nail to be found. It was put together by weaving rattan strips. This was the place where we received our first survival training crash course. We were not accustomed to that hostile environment; anyway, we learned to adjust to the life in the province interior. Our land transportation was the *paragus*, a sled pulled by water buffalo. No telephone, no refrigerator, no radio to listen to, no electricity, and no silvers to use. We could smell scents of coconut and wet rice stock. It was very pleasant after you get used to it. The breeze coming from the mountain was very pleasing, which I enjoyed the most.

In time, we got used to the call of time. It was no easy task, but we were able to blend with the requirements of time. I had seen for the first time wide rivers, crocodiles, snakes, iguanas, monkeys, komodo lizards, and many other kinds of mammals and reptiles. It was like life in Congo, Africa, as seen in the movies. When I was in Manila, the closest I was to the wild animals was from the movie screen. Living close to the river, we needed to learn how to swim. I did not know how to swim. I learned how to swim in a hurry because I had no choice; I was thrown over the side into the cold river. Later after the war, during my high school days, I became an excellent swimmer. Back in the war days, we were so naive. We did not even know how to eat with our bare hands. We were trained to use knives, spoon, and fork before the war. Therefore, we had to learn in a hurry or else get hungry. When we were in the city, I did not even like to eat vegetable. I used to say, "Vegetable is for the horse to eat only." However, during the war, I could not be choosy. I had to eat anything served on the table. Here we met our uncles, aunties, and cousins who were hiding from the Japanese. Later, we learned how to swim like dog crawl. Sometimes, I go with my uncle (Manong Bayani) to Malaylay to pick up some provisions. I remember Manong Bayani would sing on top of his lungs those beautiful Filipino love songs like "Ikaw ang Ligaya sa Buhay" and "Ang Tangi Kong Pag-ibig," as we paddled down the stream to Malaylay.

During this period, Ernesto and I were taught how to harvest rice, how to fasten *takuyan* (a woven rattan basket) around our waist, and how to properly use the *yatab* (a hand-held implement used for cutting rice straw with one hand). We picked corn and dried them and separated kernel from the cob, and we learned to cut sugarcane. We learned to plant casaba (Yucatan roots), string beans, mung beans, black pepper, bok choy, and sweet potatoes. We were very young then; however, it did not stop us from learning how to survive in time of war. I was only twelve years old, and Ernesto was eleven. We were expected to come up with something. Those were the first lessons taught to us. We were told that we had better start learning to become farmers because there was a good possibility that my father would not survive the war. Mom cried every night every time she heard those heartbreaking words.

Due to poor nutrition and contaminated water and mosquito bites, Onyoy (Jun) and I contracted malignant malaria. Malaria is a terrible sickness. One day, while on an errand, I felt a sudden chill running down my spine. I tried to control my shivering, but it became more chill. My whole body was shivering. I tried to run back, but my legs were too weak and wobbling as I tried to run. As soon as I got into the house, I lay on the straw mat and covered myself with a blanket, but that blanket was not enough to warm me. The chilling still persisted. A few minutes later, I felt sweat rolling down my spine, and my temperature rose up, way above the normal temperature. The fever was so high that I was delirious and hallucinating. I saw Teresita and Ernesto with a knife in his hand in the kitchen. I thought they were going to kill me; I darted out of the house. I was so scared of Teresita and Ernesto. I thought they were after me. Several men came to chase me and the more I got scared. I ran as fast as I could. One farmer grabbed me. I was trying to get loose but was subdued by very strong hands. He assured me that everything was all right. After an hour or two, my temperature subsided. I was given some herbal medicine. It tasted so awful. The medicine was a mixture of the juice of a plant known as sambong and of bitter melon. They boiled the leaves and then made me drink the green residue. That did not help at all.

CHAPTER 17

Mom's Intuition

After several weeks in Nagpatay, Mom decided to go to Manila to check the apartment and the stuffs we left there. Lettie and Jun accompanied her. Before leaving Mindoro, she felt that there was a good chance to meet Dad there. She had no idea of Dad's whereabouts. As far as she knew, Dad was still in Mindanao. She had no news about Dad. In spite of these thousand to one odds, she, however, brought along with her several pairs of Dad's underwear and shirts and trousers. She was almost sure that she would meet him in Manila. My father's folks were laughing upon knowing her intention; they said she must be going out of her mind. When she arrived in Manila, she went to Park Avenue to check the apartment. To her surprise, the apartment had been ransacked by looters. Nothing was left. Everything we owned were gone. Therefore, she went to her younger sister (Nicolasa), who was married to Dr. Domingo De Guzman (Tio Inggo). They had three children, namely, Domingo Jr., Nympha, and Manuel. Her sister was very ill and bedridden. Tio Inggo overheard the arrival of prisoners of war from Mindanao; he informed Nanay about his findings. And Mom without hesitation asked Tio Inggo to accompany her to meet Lieutenant Marcial Jose, her compadre. They went to a place near the staging area of prisoners of war. They went to a restaurant for refreshment. While Mom was telling them how she managed to escape to Mindoro, she noticed there were soldiers in formation in columns of two. Mom said, "Those must be the prisoners of war lined up in formation."

Lieutenant Jose interrupted and said, "No, they are Japanese soldiers."

Mom insisted that she was very sure they were not Japanese and insisted to go close enough to see them. Lieutenant Jose and Tio Inggo agreed. Mom was so excited and inquired Lieutenant Jose and Tio Inggo, "Can you see him?"

Tatay overheard her voice and said, "Narine ako." I am here.

The Japanese with fixed bayonet came to his side and said, "Kurrah, kurrah, no speak"

Mom tried to get close but was stopped by the Japanese guard. As Dad was being lined up for temporary hold in the Bilibid Prison, Dad remembered that one of his last duty in Manila was to stand as Duty Officer of the Guard in that same prison, and now he was being incarcerated in the very same prison. Their uniforms were unrecognizable; they were worn-out and torn and were unshaven, dirty and exhausted from the long trip without rest in between. Mom asked Tio Inggo to find out where they were going to take them. He informed her they would be transported in the morning to Capas, Tarlac, Concentration Camp by train, leaving from Tutuban Railway Station. Mom could not sleep that night; her mind was busy thinking of how she can get close to Dad. The following morning, she got up early and readied herself to face the great challenge of her life. Upon arriving in Tutuban Station, she went to the gate leading to the platform staging area where the prisoners of war would be assembling for embarkation. Unfortunately, she could not enter the embarkation area. She did not know what to do. However, she noticed they let the vendors selling foods in the staging area. Immediately, she went out and bought lots of puto (rice cake), bibingka (oven-cooked rice cake), and some boiled eggs. She went back to the staging area pretending as vendor; she got close to the train. Mom went to the prisoners' staging area. From where she was standing, she could not see Dad. She noticed that the side of the cattle wagon where the prisoners were kept was open about six inches to let the air into the train. She noticed that one of the many bared feet was Dad's feet. Mom inquired, "Is that you, Florencio?" Dad answered back, "Yes, it is me." Just before they talked to each other, the train whistled and started to move. Mom, catching her breath, said, "I will see you in the next train stop."

She ran back to the civilian coach that was also going to Capas. As Mom was sitting and waiting for the next train to stop, her mind was going in circles, making plans of what to do next. After a few hours that seemed to be a hundred years' wait, the train stopped, and Mom said to herself, *This is the moment I have been waiting for.* She placed herself by the exit door. As soon as the train stopped, she jumped and ran toward the stationmaster, begging him to delay the train for five minutes and then ran toward the cattle wagon where Dad was. Without hesitation, she pushed the Japanese guard out of her way and asked the prisoners of war, "Where is my husband Florencio?"

Dad was in the far end of the wagon and could not go to where Mom was standing; they raised Dad over their heads and shoulders, passed him from one person to another, and brought him right in front of Mom. With only his head hanging out the door, the short reunion was indescribable. Their sweat, tears and mucus, saliva and mixed emotion between the two were beyond my imagination. Mom was so happy to see him alive. The Japanese guard was caught by surprise and did not say anything; he was astounded with the hugging and kissing of Mom and Dad.

He just said, "Firipine no onna ii des'ne, tak'san kissu." Filipino women very good; they kiss a lot.

After that brief reunion, Mom went back to her coach and stayed there until their arrival in Capas. When the POWs disembarked the train, they formed in column of twos and boarded a truck, which took them to the Concentration Camp. Mom was not allowed to visit the POW Camp. She contacted some people who can go in and out of the camp. Only medical doctors could enter the confinement. One of them was a distant relative (Dr. Atienza) whom Mom asked to smuggle some food for Dad. After a few months, Dad got sick with appendectomy and was operated by American doctors. After a few days since the operation, the Japanese authorities allowed him to go home to recuperate with warning not to join any subversive group against the Japanese. The Japanese authority released Dad from the concentration camp on January 21, 1943. Mom accompanied Dad to provide any morale and health support. He was temporarily placed under the care of the Pampanga Provincial Hospital where he recuperated. When he was ready and able to move around without help, the Japanese authorities released him from the concentration camp. He requested to be released from the hospital. Mom and Dad together again went to Manila to pick up Lettie and Junior at Dr. Domingo de Guzman's residence. By the time they got there, it was too late for my mother to see her youngest sister alive. She passed away a few days earlier. They went straight to Mindoro via Batangas. Upon arriving in Mindoro, they proceeded to Nagpatay where he united with his children and relatives. After a few days, Mom asked Dad to move back to Pambisan because the house there was big to accommodate all of us. In Pambisan, they brought a wooden canoe (*banka*) and two offshore fish corrals (*baklad*), not very far from our house.

One summer day, my father went to Manila; he took me along with him. We took a train from Batangas to Manila. My father handed me a bag; in it were sugar and soap. As we passed the Japanese sentry, he demanded our identification papers. Father presented his, and I also presented mine. The sentry noticed that I was carrying a bag, so he demanded me to show him the bag. He then searched the bag for contraband but found nothing of interest to him. He, however, found a cake of soap and a kilo of brown sugar. He confiscated the soap and sugar and slapped my face for not presenting them to him right away. We found out later that it was illegal to transport commodity, such as sugar and soap, because they were black market items.

Japanese Soldiers inspecting train coaches

CHAPTER 18

Life in Pambisan

In early 1943, I was twelve and Ernesto eleven years old. During this part of the Japanese Occupation in the Philippines, we stayed permanently in Pambisan, a barrio in the municipality of Baco, Mindoro. Baco is an islet that measures about three miles in length and half a mile in width. In the north end is Malaylay, in the center is Baco, and in the southern part is Pambisan. It is only about three feet above sea level. It is located about five kilometers northwest of Calapan, the provincial capital of Mindoro. Pambisan had no electricity and water system. The drinking water was from underground spring and wells. The water tide level was shallow, which could easily contaminate our drinking water. Our toilet was "over yonder." The sanitary condition was very poor; it was easy to get sick, especially since our immunity was low. The people lived by catching fishes from the nearby coral and planting vegetables from the backyard gardens. They bartered their daily catch of fish for clothing and other foodstuff, such as salt and sugar. There was no milk or bread. The whole area, planted with coconut trees and some tropical fruit trees—such as lime, oranges, avocados, guavas, jackfruit, pineapple, mangoes, atis, and santol—was an ideal place to live in at that time.

We had an abundance of fish, fruits, and vegetables. Our rice was coming from our rice field in Bayanan; we had tenants taking care of the rice field and the corn we harvested from Nagpatay. We raised some pigs and chicken. We stayed in the house of my late grandfather (Lolo Martin Samaco). Lolo

Martin was a seafaring merchant; he was very successful in his business. He transported lumbers from the Philippines to Yokohama, Japan, before the war in his two-masted sailboat. His sailboat was named after his three daughters, *Tres hermanas* (three sisters). Unfortunately, he perished during a heavy typhoon off China Sea, in the northwest of Mindoro in February 7, 1939. No survivors were found. The house he left was so big that we used to play ball in the living room; it had four big bedrooms, and the dining area and kitchen were, together, the whole width of the house. From a bird's-eye view, it looked like an L shape. The house itself was made of fine Philippine narra, tindalo, and dao lumbers—a rarity now. The windows were made of fine wood framing with 2½ by 2½ inch capiz seashell. The stairs were of narra wood about 2 inches in thickness by 6 feet in length and 12 inches in width. The floor was elevated about 10 feet high from the ground and made of 18 inches wide by 1 inch thick. The furnishing—such as beds, dining table, living room set, and upright dressers—were made of solid black dao. We were very fortunate because the huge estate that he left supported us during the entire duration of the Japanese occupation. There was an abundance of food, and we never got hungry. We had plenty of rice, corn, coconuts, and bananas. We had chickens, pigs, and seafood. We were very lucky to have a mother who knew what was best for us. At that same time in Manila where we came from, people were dying of starvation. Mom's advance planning was perfect. Had we stayed in Manila, it could have been impossible for us to survive. In Pambisan, we even had fiesta and Flores de Mayo (Flower of May Festival).

Ernesto and I learned to mend bamboo fish traps using *danlay* and *ugnay* (bamboo rounded stick and vines). Mom became a gourmet specialist on seafood like adobo sa gata igat (eel cooked in coconut milk), shark, and other denizens of the deep. Sometimes, Ernesto and I would accompany Dad for deep-sea clam harvesting. Tatay and I dove, collected the clams from the sea floor, and placed them in the basket while Ernesto hauled them up and emptied them in the canoe.

Dad was very innovative. He designed a coconut press and *kabyawan* (coconut meat-shredding machine). The device was made of a wooden shaft with one end a ball shape, the blade section a sawtooth-like blade, and the body was the pulley. It was resting on two wooden pillow blocks on each end. In the middle part of the shaft, a rope wound twice around it, and the ends of the rope attached to the ends of two—to three-feet-long bamboo poles, with ends fastened loosely to form a pivot. These bamboo poles acted as pedals that drive the shaft to turn on its axis clockwise and counterclockwise. The husked coconuts cut in halves were then pushed against the shredder shaft, held and guided by two hands of the operator. Ernesto and I learned to operate the device. It did not take long for us to learn. A quota of one hundred shredded coconuts was to be finished before we can play. By the time we finished, we were much tired and did not feel like playing anymore. Before we started shredding the coconut, we had to lay out several corrugated galvanized iron sheets under the sun in the courtyard. The shredded coconut meat was spread evenly on the hot corrugated sheet. At the end of the day when the sun set, the shredded coconut turns to dark brown in color because of the heat from the sun and the corrugated sheet holding it. The water content had evaporated, leaving nothing but oil in the coconut meat. The waterless coconut would then be placed into several rattan baskets and then placed in the horizontal press for oil extraction. The whole process was done without the use of fire, except the heat from the sun (now we call solar energy).

From the coconut tree, Dad produced alcohol, sugar, soap, vinegar, wine, and oil. Our drinking cups and kitchen utensil were from coconut hard shell. Our glass were made from empty bottles cut in half. To do this, we simply poured fresh water into the bottle until it reached the desired height. Then we squirt a drop or two of oil, just enough to make a very thin sheet of oil on top of the water. With a one-forth-inch iron rod formed to a ring in the end having a diameter slightly bigger than that of the bottle, the rod was then heated cherry red-hot and then carefully placed and aligned with the area where the oil was located, and in few seconds, the bottle would snap. This was due to the differential temperature of the oil and water. The edges were then honed against the sand to remove sharp edges. We use this glass for drinking and for oil lamps by fastening a piece of rolled cotton cloth by a wire, which served as the wick.

During bad weathers, like *habagat* and *amihan* (monsoon season), the *baklad* (fish corral) would always suffer damages. We replaced the fish corrals' post; this was a very difficult repair work because while piling down the post, the canoe where we were standing kept on swaying, caused by current and heavy wind. It was hard to keep balance, especially on top of the canoe without outriggers. At times, it rained heavily, and the canoe would roll and pitch, making it much harder to make repairs. With much patience and perseverance, we were able to make the necessary repairs. Though it was a hard life, we never go to sleep with empty stomach. We had a good catch of different kinds of fishes: *matang baka, samaral, dalagang bukid, sap-sap*, red snapper, and many more. We also caught lots of shellfishes, shrimps, and crabs. We also had our gelatins from seaweeds called gulaman. Mom cooked eels boiled in coconut milk and some leaves. During nice weathers, we planted some coconuts and cassava. It was not an easy life, but we were a happy family in spite of the war. We learned how to drink coconut wine, *tuba*; when unfermented and fresh from the tree, it was very tasty and sweet. It is so sweet that anyone might keep on drinking without knowing it can make him or her drunk. The fermented tuba is very strong. They used some kind of bark called *tangal* to help ferment it to its alcohol level. We also had rice crispies we called *pinipig*. It is made from a very young rice grain that are still green. The grains flatten by pounding in a *lusong* (wooden hollow) with a *bayo* (heavy wooden bat). The grains flatten and separate from the shell. The pinipig is then roasted and served with coconut milk. Our cookies were made from rice or cassava flour; they called them *puto seko*. Our *merienda* or snack were *puto* (steamed ground-rice cake), *ginataan* (a combination of banana, sweet potato, jack fruit, corn, taro roots, and sweet rice boiled together in coconut milk), *bibinka* (rice cake cooked over and under burning wood charcoal), *sinulbut* (square banana cooked in boiling sugar molasses), *maja blanca* (corn cake), and *gulaman* (a jello made from seaweeds). When we were short of rice grain, the corn grain or green banana cube was added to increase the volume.

Our medicine was from herbs and fruit tree leaves like guava leaves boiled in water and used as antiseptic for all kinds of cuts, sores and bruises, stomachaches, and enema. It was also good for the newly circumcised and for bathing a newly born baby. The dried avocado leaves were also boiled and served as tea. Our medicine for malaria was derived from cinchona bark; the bark is boiled in water, and the residue of which was used as medicine. That was Tatay's idea. He, being a chemist, knew how and where the medicines were extracted. An example was quinine, a malaria medicine made from the cinchona bark after boiling. That medicine cured me from malignant malaria.

We made our own toys, like sailboat from coconut husk and dried coconut bosoms. Our softball was from old socks rolled together to form a ball. A real softball—it was really a soft ball. Our playhouse was made of coconut palm leaves stashed together on a bamboo pole. The boys' pastime was playing *basagan*, smashing two seashells together; the boy with the shell that stayed intact was the winner. We also played our war games; we fashioned our guns called sumpak. This *sumpak* is made out of a thick-walled bamboo tube; the hole inside the bamboo is about one-fourth inch in diameter with both ends open. A rounded coconut meat is inserted tightly through one end, and a bamboo pushrod with brushy end is inserted into the hole, which builds up pressure and ejects the coconut projectile at high speed when the pushrod is suddenly pushed. Very similar to the principle of air gun.

On early evenings, we gathered at the beach, and while waiting for our storyteller, we played *suong*, similar to the Japanese sumo. We drew a circle on the sand; in the middle of the circle were two boys with their hands around each other's waist and throw the opponent out of the circle. When the storyteller showed up to tell us some horror stories, we listened intently in wild imagination until goose bumps showed. We felt a sudden chill on our back. After listening to the horror stories, we go back to our homes. It was pitch dark and quiet; at times, we hear the barking dogs. We were so scared, always thinking of the horror stories. I almost would like to run as if the thing we were scared of was right behind us—the *kapre*, a tall black man with two horns on top of his head and burning eyes and a goat-looking long legs. The kapre sits on the branch of a big banyan tree, smoking a big cigar and scaring people passing by. One night, I left early. I went under one of the bully kid's house and waited for him. As soon as he climbed the bamboo open stairs, I grabbed his legs, and the poor guy cried out in fear. Many times, I would enjoy just sitting on the beach. Tasting the spray of salty water from the rolling waves that slammed against the rocks on the shore. Feeling the cool breeze coming from the sea that touched my face while listening to the sound of the rushing waves slamming against the seashore and the sound of the swaying coconut palm leaves. It was a very soothing feeling, especially after a day's hard work, to listen to the musical sound of nature, which hypnotized me until I fell asleep. I sometimes watched the silhouette of passing Japanese naval ship slowly coming up from the horizon. The smell of seawater and the spray of saltwater on my lips were very satisfying. And the sweet smell of *dama de noche* and the amorous smell of citrus flowers completed the day. There were instances I mentally daydreamed those past years in Pambisan. Sitting down on the black sandy beach, I watched the flickering lights from the silhouette of distant Japanese ship steaming far out near the horizon and the returning anglers with their catch for the day. Sometimes in the evening, I tagged along with older boys; they wore their best with a guitar sling hanging around their necks, off to serenade (*harana*) the girls of their choice. While one was playing the guitar and the others sing a romantic song, the lady they were serenading would open the window pane and place an oil lamp by the windowsill and sit by the window. Later the father or mother of the lady would ask them to come in and let them get themselves acquainted. Life was very simple. No electricity—we used oil lamp *perok-perok* or on special occasion Coleman alcohol lamp. No faucet—our water supply was from the wells and manual pumps connected to subterranean water spring. The water tasted funny, but we got used to it. During this time, Mom lost a baby by miscarriage. Ernesto and I buried the miscarried fetus in the backyard. Later, Mila, our ninth sibling, was born.

On or about May 1943, I got sick with dysentery. I lost lots of weight, and my mother was told that I would die soon. Mom cried upon learning this news. I sensed that my condition was getting worse; however, I told Mom not to worry. I said to her, "I am going to be strong again and be around for a long time to help and play."

That day the barrio folks were celebrating their patron saint. I, being very ill, tried to sit down by the window to witness the occasion down in the courtyard. The men played softball, waxed bamboo pole climbing contest, on top of the pole was a fresh green coconut with coins buried onto the surface of the husk, also tug-of-war, and many more. At the seashore, the water was calm. I saw they would fashion a ten feet by fifteen feet bamboo raft with a small shed covered with coconut palm leaves and all the trimmings and decorations from coconut leaves and bamboo. On board, there was a small group of musicians equipped with brass musical instrument, drums, and guitars, playing their best. Outrigger boats and canoes were all around it as the raft floated on the sea. It was a great feeling when I saw people get together in harmony as if there was no war going on. After a whole day of excitement, they continued the celebration well on to the night. They formed two long columns of young boys and girls, followed by women and men dressed in their best. Now, I sometimes think how they managed to have those fancy dress at the time of war. They were carrying bamboo torch. In the middle of the column was the patron saint carried on a bamboo platform on their shoulders by most able young men, followed by the *Reyna Elena* (Queen Elena) and her escort. As they paraded around the town, they sang the church hymn "Dios de Salve Maria" (Mary Mother of God the Savior) and "Santa Maria Madre de Dios" (Saint Mary Mother of God). They called this celebration Flores de Mayo (Flowers of May). After the procession, they assembled in front of the makeshift chapel, casting flowers around and at the patron saint as they sing the Gospel. Later, they proceeded to the platform where the Reyna Elena was seated and crowned. Standing by her side was her escort who I believe was Ernesto, my younger brother. I too had a part, but due to my illness, somebody replaced me. Many of my playmates came over to visit me and gave me morale booster. Fortunately, with the help of the medicine *sulfathiasol* given by Dr. Infantado of Calapan, I survived and finally recovered from that dreadful illness. One day, I hurt myself when I was wearing a wooden clog. I tripped and accidentally kicked a rock; my toenail was uprooted. I suffered for many days. I could not walk; it became so bad and smelled bad that I was afraid it might lead to gangrene. I again went to see Dr. Infantado. Without anesthetic, he pulled my toenail. It was very painful, but after that, the pain subsided. That was my last illness to this day. Thanks to God for keeping me away from any serious illness.

During this time, Tatay was very busy attending to his small fishing business and, of course, to his family; and every now and then, he would go up to the interior, providing intelligence assistance to the guerrilla movement. Though he was inducted as Captain in the U.S. Army Forces Far East (USAFFE), he was not readily accepted by the Filipino guerrillas because of his surrendering to the Japanese Imperial Army. He did not have any other option but to obey his Commanding General to lay down his arms and surrender.

He made several attempts to join the guerrilla forces but was turned down because he was an ex-POW and also because the guerrilla commanding officer was afraid that Dad might outrank him. Tatay even asked them to give him a lower rank, but they were afraid they might have a conflict. In spite of their denial, Tatay provided them with pertinent information on the Japanese movements in the area. On several occasions, he put his family in narrow escape from danger. He made contact with the guerrillas. We were living at a very close proximity from the Japanese Garrison, only five kilometers away. The only thing that made the delay in their arrival to our vicinity was the river separating us from the main land; the river was about a kilometer wide. It was necessary to board a canoe before they could land on our shore, and we were given an advance warning by the barangay association. This gave us ample time to make preparations for their arrival. The Japanese authorities initiated this barangay association as a lookout for the incoming guerrillas; it turned out the opposite. They were the lookout for the oncoming Japanese arrival to give advance warning of approaching danger of the Japanese reconnaissance patrol.

There were many instances we had narrow escapes. One of them was during the time when Dad was away saving the life of the wife and daughter of a guerrilla leader (Captain Beloncio). This Captain Beloncio had an intention of rescuing his wife and daughter from the Japanese Garrison. Dad, upon learning about this plan, contacted Captain Beloncio, and volunteered to rescue them instead of the guerrilla attacking the Japanese

Garrison. Dad was so worried that should Captain Beloncio and his troops attack the Japanese Garrison in Calapan, the Japanese would retaliate to the people of Calapan, and they would be at the mercy of the Japanese hands or there might be a massacre as had been experienced before in other towns. The civilians suffered. Captain Beloncio agreed and gave his assurance that he would not go ahead with his plan with the condition that Dad would rescue Captain Beloncio's wife and daughter. My father virtually saved Calapan from massacre. He also did save the mother and daughter and brought them before the Captain at his hideout. He did save not only the mother and daughter, but also the lives of the innocent people of Calapan where the Garrison was located.

Decapitation of farmer in Malaylay

While he was engaged in saving the lives of the wife and daughter of the guerrilla leader, we could be in danger ourselves, his family. The Guerrillas from the other band ambushed a platoon of Japanese reconnaissance patrol; several Japanese soldiers were killed while crossing the river in Malaylay. The others fled and made their way back to their garrison where they informed the incident to the garrison commander. The Japanese commander sent out a company of troopers to hunt the guerrillas. The guerrillas, however, were gone. They were back to their farming chores. (This reminds me of the Vietnamese peasants who turned Vietcong in their pajama-looking clothing) The Japanese soldiers, not being able to find the guerrillas, were frustrated and turned their frustration to the innocent civilians. The Japanese soldiers, receiving information given by the spy or collaborators that the farmers were the guerrillas too, interrogated all males from ages sixteen and older they came across. Those who were not able to give them a satisfactory answer were seized, bound, and taken along to carry their provisions. The others had their hands tied on their backs with the other end of the rope around the neck of the person behind him. On their way, they arrested about fifty, and when they arrived in Malaylay, they dug a pit barely two feet deep and, without hesitation, commenced executing them by beheading one after another as they kneeled in front of their grave. The officers and noncom were the ones executing the decapitation. Some who got tired of beheading gave samurai sword to some enlisted; some did not like to participate but were ordered to do so or face disobedience to orders. With a lightning thrust of the *katana* samurai sword, the body was decapitated, and the head rolled like coconut fruit on the ground. The headless torso fell on the ground, and the hands reflexed almost like a fish when the head was suddenly cut-off. The body flipped up and down. One private was ordered to decapitate one of the prisoners; he refused to do so. The noncom reprimanded him and said, "If do not do as ordered you will be charge of disobedience." Hesitantly, he followed; the noncom handed him the samurai sword, he gripped the sword, his hands shaking, and he froze. The noncom kicked his butt; only then did he raise the sword and struck the neck with closed eyes. He did not cut clean, and the noncom kicked his butt again and shouted at him, "Bakayaro." It was a gruesome sight. Some who were reluctant to do such horrible act missed to cut completely, and the head was partially cut. During the whole process, only one got away; he was told to climb the coconut tree to push down the young coconut. The Japanese soldiers, being weary and worn out, sat down to refresh themselves; they drank the coconut juice. They were so thirsty and got themselves busy. The man who climbed stayed up the tree and did not make any move until the Japanese forgot about him up there on the top of the coconut tree. He slowly slid down the tree trunk; as soon as he touched the ground, he ran and ran toward the mangrove, not minding the crocodile-infested swamp. He swam through the river and across to the deep jungle until he reached the mountain top and was given shelter by the Mangyans (aborigines). He stayed there until the end of the war; he went down because he saw a company of Japanese soldiers going up the mountain,. He was afraid that they were after him. He did not know that the Japanese were now stragglers hiding from the American and Filipino soldiers. However, the twenty-five of the fifty prisoners were spared for a short time to carry their provisions back to the garrison. I witnessed this atrocity. The execution took place about two hundred feet away from me. I was hiding in the attic of my grandmother's house where I had a clear view of the whole events. I wanted to cry but did not for fear that they might hear me. Some were not buried; they left the bodies for the crocodiles to eat. When the troopers returned from their reconnaissance expedition, there were but twenty-five civilian captives with them. The provision was gone so with the civilian carrying them. They took the rest of the twenty-five on board a motorboat and executed them at sea.

One day while we were playing hide-and-seek on the beach, one of my playmates called our attention. He was shivering and was as white as a ghost. He told us he saw a dead man bubbling on the beach. We were curious, so we went to see, and all of us got scared. The head, still attached to the body, was partly floating in the water. We ran home and informed our parents of what we just saw. They (our parents) went there to see for themselves; they picked up the body, and they identified him as one of the farmers from Malaylay, and then they took the body to Malaylay to the victim's relatives and buried it by the nipa swamp. The guerrillas, however, had their own way of atrocity; when they catch a Japanese soldier, they instead cut their organ and stuck it in their mouth. Sometimes they cut the meat part of the legs and stuck it in the soldiers' mouth before they kill them. Atrocity was on both sides of the fence. On one instance, a guerrilla beheaded a captured Japanese officer; the guerrilla hung the head by his waist to show to his superior of his prize. And while crossing a cold river, the head, whose mouth was open, suddenly bit his behind because of the reflexes as it submerged in cold water. They had to pry open the mouth with a bayonet. The guerrillas did their own beheading with their bolos. The Japanese were scared of the guerrillas. They never walked alone; they always had partners anytime they step out of the garrison. I guess that was the reason why they became trigger-happy; however unknown to us, their training and instruction was to kill if possible no prisoners.

One day Dad and I went to Manila. I do not know for what reason. On our way to the city, we boarded a train from Batangas. When we arrived in Tutuban Train Station in Manila, we were in a hurry to get out of the train station because Dad was already late to meet his military buddies. I was carrying a bag full of several items: soap, sugar, and rice. As we passed through the sentry, the guard told me to open the bag so that he can inspect it. I opened the bag; he found the sugar and soap. Those items were high commodity items. Some people black-market them. The guard slapped me across the face, kicked me, and then confiscated the bag. My father could not do anything but look on as the guard was slapping me.

At one instance, I was passing by the sentry, and I forgot to say, "Ohayo." The guard called back, shouting, "Kurah, kurah." He made a bowing gesture and said, "Ohayo." I did as told, but instead, I said "Ohayop," meaning "you animal" in Filipino. He kicked my butt for not greeting him.

CHAPTER 19

Close Call

One summer night, we received unexpected visitors from Manila. There were five of them. One of them was a good friend of my dad; he was Captain Benito Ebuen, Air Corps. He was the leader of the group. The others were Lieutenant Joe Rogers, Air Corps (AC); Lieutenant Punsalan, AC; Lieutenant Ortiz, AC; and Philippine Military Academy Cadet Isidro Abad. They were escapees and wanted by the Japanese authority. They were on their way to Panay Island to catch a submarine for Australia. They wound up staying with us for about a year. During their stay, we were very careful of our actions and kept our lips tight and sealed. There were several Japanese collaborators in the area. Fortunately, none of them reported us to the Japanese.

I guess Dad knew how to deal with them that was why we were not reported to the Japanese authorities.

One night while Dad was out with the five wanted officers, one Japanese noncommissioned officer—a *Kempetai*, equivalent to German Gestapo—suddenly showed up at our house. He was Fujihara. Fujihara came by to see what was going on in our locality. My father, a former prisoner of war, was checked occasionally, to ensure he was not making contact or joining the guerrilla movement. That was the reason he went directly to our house. He inquired Mom, "Where is Captain Medina?"

Mom replied, "He went to the countryside to get some rice and vegetables for his family."

She continued, "You see, we have many children, and our food provision is almost exhausted."

Fujihara was making his pace with a dangling samurai sword hanging by his waist in front of Mom. While pacing back and forth, he noticed a row of five beds, lined up side by side in the north side of our living room.

He asked Mom, "Medina san, why you havu five bedu in riving room?"

Mom said, "We have many children. They have to sleep far apart so that if one gets sick, the other may not get it. You see hard to get medicine nowadays."

Fujihara said, "Oh, I understand."

While he was pacing back and forth in front of Mom while questioning, Mom noticed there was a new aviation magazine on top of the table by the window. She slowly switched her position and stood in front of the table to conceal the magazine, beads of sweat were on her forehead. The Kempetai did not notice her scared face or the magazine, maybe, because of the poor lighting. The Kempetai left and went to our neighbor whom he liked to visit. She was a pretty young lady, half Spanish. Her name was Puri. When he saw her, he asked her if he knew where Captain Medina was. She told him most probably he went to the field to get some provision for his family.

CHAPTER 20

Our Last Close Encounter with the
Japanese Soldiers

One night in October 1944, about six in the evening, a week before the arrival of the American Liberating Forces, Dad sent me to deliver a message to Malaylay guerrilla contact. On my way there, I saw a large number of Filipino guerrillas led by an American. They were all dressed in combat fatigue uniform and well armed, unlike those ragtag guerrillas I used to see. The new uniform looked funny; their pants and shirt pockets were oversized it looked like buggy pants. The helmets looked oversized too, and their shoes were heavy combat boots. Some wore leggings made of canvas laced together on the side of each leg. Their sidearms were .30-caliber carbine, Garand rifles, Browning automatic rifles (BAR), semiautomatic carbines, grease guns, and Thompson submachine guns. Hand grenades were dangling, hanging on their service belts along with mess kits and canteens. They were carrying the provision—half of a whole cow's meat strung on a bamboo pole carried by two men on each end of the pole. Upon seeing this, I immediately turned back and ran toward home to inform Dad of the incoming guerrillas. Few minutes later, I saw Dad talking with the guerrilla leader. They knew each other. The leader's name was Captain William Dodson. He was a mining engineer before the war broke out. When the Japanese invaded the Philippines, he joined the guerrilla movement. They talked about the war and the news of the liberating army, that America was winning the war. The tide has reversed its flow. Captain Dodson told Dad of their mission. He informed him that they were the advance party and were going to intercept the retreating Japanese army. While they were making their plans, the soldiers were busy preparing their food. They cooked a portion of the cow's meat and one sack of rice and some vegetables. There were no plates or fork or spoon; they ate with their bare hands. Banana leaves laid on the table to serve as plates. The rice was placed on top of the banana leaves. It was a big mess. After their dinner, they relaxed and smoked American cigarettes and chewed gums. They gave us dried peaches, apricots, and chocolate bars with an inscription on the wrapper: "I shall return—Gen. Douglas MacArthur." After dinner, they told stories about their many Japanese encounters. They each started saying their favorite jokes, and then they retired. The officers slept in our living room and the enlisted men on the ground floor.

On the following day at about seven o'clock in the morning, the troops called to assemble fell in line in our courtyard in front of our house. The officers called the roll and then gave each soldier yellow tablets, an "atabrine tablet" for malaria. After which, they marched toward a place named Punta where they boarded several outriggers to cross the river. Dad accompanied them to the other side, which I believe was Baruyan.

After they left our premises, the whole place was a shamble—empty cigarette wrappers of Chesterfield, Lucky Strike, Piedmont; chewing gums and chocolate wrappings were all scattered all over the place. By looking at the place, there was no way a person could deny the presence of guerrilla troopers. Fortunately, the neighbors came by and picked up the scattered empty cigarette wrappers for their souvenirs. We saved some chocolate bars for the later days.

It was about nine o'clock in the morning. Dad just arrived and was resting from his short trip, a messenger sent by the Barangay Neighborhood Association came running and informed Dad of the Japanese Troopers on their way crossing the river. It was such luck; the guerrillas went on the direction slightly off the direction where the Japanese troopers were coming from. Dad was thinking that the activities the night before and its consequences should the Japanese find out we were harboring guerrillas could mean a certain death to all of us. The five wanted officers forced themselves to climb the coconut trees; they learned to climb coconut palm trees in no time. They were all up on the coconut trees, hiding and not making any sound. Dad told us to eat all the chocolate bars and burn the wrappers and anything that could lead us to our destruction. A radio transmitter-receiver was hidden in the embankment covered with coconut palm leaves. The barrio people were all running away, carrying with them their few belongings wrapped in bed sheets. In no time, the whole neighborhood was deserted; they all ran for the mountain and swamp. It made us feel eerie. The only people left were Grandpa Lucio and his family. All our neighbors had vacated their houses and fled to the hills for fear the Japanese might massacre the whole barrio. They knew massacre could happen just like that in our neighboring town where all men, young and old, were rounded up and herded like cattle going to be slaughtered into a schoolhouse and padlocked. They then poured gasoline around the building and set them on fire. Guards with fixed bayonets standing around the building shot anyone who tried to escape. Our neighbors were afraid. This time we would all be slaughtered, and it was known to them that there were several Japanese collaborators in the barrio who could have informed the Japanese.

We braced ourselves for the worse, thinking we probably ran out of luck. In the past years, we were very fortunate we escaped several narrow escapes. At that moment, Mom was doing her rosary, as usual every time we were facing imminent danger. The whole barrio was quiet, and everything seemed to stand still. Even the wind and the swaying of the leaves of the coconut palm trees seemed to stop—a feeling like when a typhoon is about to come.

Few minutes have gone by and a platoon of Japanese soldiers appeared with their nambu rifle in fixed bayonets led by a young officer with his samurai sword dangling around his waist. They first surrounded Grandpa Lucio's house. His dogs were barking at the soldiers, but Grandpa Lucio could not stop the barking because he could not call his dogs' names. He named his dogs after the Japanese Generals and MacArthur—Homma, Tojo, and Douglas.

While the Japanese were at Grandpa Lucio's house, Dad said to us, "This is it." But he assured us not to worry; we would be okay. The Japanese soldiers surrounded our house, all in fixed bayonets. The Japanese leader approached Dad and greeted him, saying, "Ohayo." Good Morning.

Dad responded with, "Ohayo gozaimas." And continued, "What brings you here?"

The Japanese officer said in perfect English, "I was told that there was a big celebration here last night. I can see from the appearance of your courtyard. I want to know what the activity was all about."

Dad smiled and said, "Oh, yes, indeed, we had a big party last night. It was my youngest son's birthday. Sorry, we were not able to invite you." Just before the Japanese were about to ask another question, Augusto (my

KELLY S. MEDINA

youngest brother), who was only six years old, stood on the windowsill, with a proud face looked down at the Japanese troopers, and began singing the Japanese Favorite Army song, "Miyotou O kaino." While Augusto was singing, Dad took advantage of the situation and said to the Japanese officer, "Oh, yes, that's him up there singing. It was his birthday last night." The most interesting part about this happening was that. Augusto, who always sang "God Bless America," suddenly sang the Japanese song. The Japanese soldiers joined him, and after singing, they all hailed, "Banzai! Banzai!"

After this, our nervousness and tension calmed down, and all were smiling. Dad then ordered me to bring a pitcher of water and some bananas for the soldiers. In my excitement, I pulled my hands from my pocket, and by accident, I dropped the message I was supposed to deliver to the guerrilla contact in Malaylay the previous night. The Japanese soldier picked it up without reading and gave to me. I took it from his hand as if it was nothing important, just a piece of paper. Nobody paid attention for the Japanese to be aware. The Japanese officer then confided to Dad their real purpose for their sudden visit to our barrio.

He said to Dad, "Captain Medina, we are looking for a sailboat to commandeer that could take us to Lubang Island, do you have any?"

He continued in a low tone of voice, "The Americans have landed in San Jose last week in October, and we are in need a way of getting out of here." Of course, Dad did not show a sigh of relief but informed the officer that we had two sailboats, but they were under repair. The boat needed to be caulked, and it would take about one week to get them dried and launched. Definitely, it could not be put on water in a very short time. The Japanese did not insist to carry it out anyway. The Japanese, not being able to obtain what they sought, left and went back to their garrison in Calapan. That was our last encounter with the Japanese, except after the war in 1957 when I joined the U.S. Navy and, finally, was caught by the Japanese while stationed in Sasebo, Japan. I got married to a Japanese (Sayoko). I was imprisoned with her for thirty-eight years in Japan and the United States.

After that last encounter, we were all looking up at the sky, watching Japanese and American planes doing dogfights. Stray .50-caliber bullets were falling around us; we did not mind at all. We just took cover under the coconut palm trees. It seemed as if nothing could happen to us; our liberator was just around the corner. Later, we watched the leaflets falling down coming from the American plane passing by. It was addressed to the Japanese soldiers asking them to surrender. Just before the arrival of the American Liberating Forces, some of our relatives were not quite lucky.

116

For one instance, one of our distant relative, Uncle Garce Lualhati, was caught hiding an automatic pistol; he was suspected as a guerrilla. They interrogated him severely, but without effect. They then tied his arms and body and feet together after which they hung him upside down and lifted his body twelve inches above the floor and then let go of the rope, causing his head to ram against the concrete floor. Seeing that they could not obtain the information they sought from him, they then dragged him to the bridge and then lowered him into the water until close to being drowned and finally killed him by thrusting a bayonet on his back. Another relative, a dentist, was subjected to torture—our late uncle Jesus Punzalan. He and his wife, our late Tia Toping, and their youngest daughter were incarcerated in the Japanese garrison. They were tortured because the Japanese believed they conspired with the guerrillas. The interrogator made Uncle Jesus drink as much water as they could pour into his mouth, gallon after gallon of water, until he was close to drowning, and then they placed a long wooden plank on top of his belly while lying on his back, and they then had two soldiers sit on each end of the plank as if they were seesawing. Later, they were spared and released for lack of evidence, lucky for them. After the war, our old-time neighbor in Camp Murphy told us that their father, Lieutenant Alberto Llanes, was tortured and murdered by launching at him with a bayonet right in front of his wife and children. I could not imagine those horrible sight and experience.

As the American forces got closer to the Philippines, the Japanese became so mean, and they retaliated to the civilians anytime they hear they were losing grounds. For instance, in Manila, civilians were caught between the artillery bombardment of the American forces coming from the south and from the north. And while this was happening, the Japanese took a potshot on any civilians they saw on the street, regardless of their age and sex. The sniper shot any civilian running and crossing the street. Some civilians had to fetch water from the broken pipes. They had to cross the street to get some water, and in doing so, snipers shot most of them. The Japanese marines would round up as many males around their vicinity as they could. They made them stand before a wall and raked them with machine guns. One Japanese soldier was rolling a drum of gasoline to be used for burning their arsenal. As he passed by the air raid shelter, he saw civilians hiding in the shelter. Instead of taking the gasoline to the arsenal, he rolled it into the air raid shelter and shot the gasoline drum, which burst into flames. Men, women, and children were crying from pain; some got out of the shelter but were shot as they came out. They died with bullet holes and were consumed by fire. They rounded up young women from ages twelve to eighteen. They took them in one school building, and they took turns in raping them. One woman later said that she became their comfort woman; she had twenty-three soldiers in one day that had sex with her. She did not have time to rest. The soldiers were told that they had better do this because when the Americans would come, they would do the same to their women in Japan.

CHAPTER 21

Why Japanese Atrocity

In 1957, I enlisted in the United States Navy. Two years later, I was stationed in transport ship whose home port in the Far East was Yokohama, Japan. The first time I met the Japanese people, I was impressed with the way they welcomed us. They were very polite, honest, and very hospitable. I could not believe my eyes when I saw the way they treated us. I guess at the time, they probably treated us nicely because we were nice to them or maybe because we were their conquerors. But I don't think that may be the case. I truly believed they were good citizens of their country—clean and well mannered in all respect. They were such a happy people in spite of their defeat and hardship after they lost in the war. They did not take revenge against the occupation forces. They respected the surrender to America with honesty and truthfulness. I would like to look back and see what caused the change of their mentality during their occupation in other countries.

Looking back in Japanese history from the time of Emperor Meiji, the Japanese common people were subjected to many forms of inhuman treatment, which to Western civilization were barbaric in nature. As Emperor, Meiji declared himself sacred and inviolable, head of the empire, supreme commander of armed forces, and superintendent of all sovereignty. He was the source of all law emanating in that government and could dismiss any official that did not agree with him. The people had no right because they were not even citizens; they were called *shimnin,* meaning people who obey orders from the emperor without question. After Meiji died, Taisho inherited the throne and continued the same Meiji policies. Japan showed the world that they can do what Western countries can do. They proved it by invading China and defeating Russia. They introduced to their people the *Yamato damashii*, also known as spirit warrior. Taisho had a son, Hirohito, who was trained in military tactics and military government. For his early education, he was subjected to complete military discipline; his instructors were retired generals and admirals. Because Japan needed divine guidance, Hirohito was made a living god. "The emperor was regarded as a god, and therefore, they had to obey whatever the emperor said," said Teruko Tabata. The soldiers were put or subjected to the utmost training, which included degrading a person to the lowest a human could ever imagine. In the eyes of an officer, the soldier was worth no more than a *yen*. They kicked and slapped for no reason. The officers were classed as warlords: they thought of themselves as samurai, which they were not. Samurai was an honorable title; they served their *townsmen* according to their code of honor, the Bushido. If they failed to do their task, they killed themselves by committing *seppuku* or hara-kiri or cutting their guts. Samurai lived by their *Bushido Code*, which literally means Military-Knight-Ways. The ways that fighting nobles observed in their daily lives and followed in their work. The code was a moral rule of the warrior class. This warrior class produced a distinct type of mind and character that was very expressive of the national character. Bushido, therefore, was a moral rule that the samurai had to follow. They were honest, worthy, selfless, and fearless in battle. It was an unspoken written law found only in the heart of man.

Where and when it started is not known to this day. They, however, most probably began during the feudal ages in twelfth century during the Yoritomo period. Samurai was a class warrior, and it meant an attendant and guard serving under a Lord or Tonosama. In the early stage of the Samurai, they were unruly, rugged, and with no moral codes. As time went by, the Tonosama began to regulate the behavior of the Samurai. Since they were always fighting, they needed some measures by which they were to be judged, such as fair play in fighting with other clan. However, in the later years, the so-called warrior spirits were taught brutality, no compassion. The field regulation of the Japanese army were said to be from the Bushido. However, with major changes, they bastardized the Bushido in the form of the *Yamato damashii* way.

Bushido code is actually not the way some people think about it. The Bushido teaching was to be kind to their prisoner and give them the necessary assistance when injured. Killing and torture was the name of the game. To die for their emperor was the greatest contribution they could give their country. During the occupation of Nanking, China, hundreds of Chinese were held in a warehouse to be used as object for bayonet practice by enlisted men. One noncommissioned officer reported to his superior officers that they had enough material for bayonet practice. For the officers, it was mandatory to chop off heads of captive Chinese; this was one of their proficiency for advancement. In Nanking, about one-third of the city was gutted by fire. More than twenty thousand Chinese male civilians of military age were marched out of the city and massacred with bayonets or machine guns. Many women and young girls were raped, murdered, and then mutilated. Older persons were robbed and shot. By the end of the month, at least twenty thousand or more civilians had been slaughtered. A Japanese army recruit had to undergo a severe punishment where he was pummeled, slapped, kicked, and beaten daily by their immediate superior without apparent reason. For swimming training, if he did not know how to swim, he would be tied around his waist with a rope and thrown out to the water; they would leave him in the water until he learned. If he got almost drowned, he would raised to be revived and thrown again until he learned how to swim. During bayonet launching practice, a two-inch red mark was placed on the chest of a Chinese prisoner to indicate the heart's location; however, the location of the heart was not the target. The trainee had to avoid the heart so that they can use the body for a longer period. One officer, Nishihara san, a college graduate of University of Tokyo, reported that during his indoctrination, some of the junior officers were called outside to witness the beheading of a Chinese prisoner, and later they were told to do the same. The first time he attempted to do it, he was shaking or trembling all over his body; he could not grasp the sword, and the instructor scolded him for not being a man. He was forced to do so. His mind went blank and a sudden thrust of the sword chopped off the head, and he saw it rolling about three feet from him; he was handed with a white cloth to wipe off the dripping blood from the blade of his sword. After the killing, he felt a strange sensation in his system as if he lost his soul, and he felt like a superhuman and like the devil. As he looked at some of the soldiers before the killing, their eyes seemed evil-looking, sharp, and burning red; and now after he killed the man by the sword, he noticed that the soldiers didn't have evil eyes anymore because he himself became the devil with evil eyes. Some soldiers had visible scars on their faces; as a recruit, they had been beaten constantly. They slapped them, and sometimes, they used their leather slippers when their hands hurt from slapping. One recruit's parents were so happy to send their only son, Masahiro Tanaka, to the recruit training for the benevolent emperor's military. "During his basic training," he recalled, "my head was beaten with fresh bamboo poles and my face slapped with leather slippers. My face was disfigured by this, my parent will not recognize me, and I wonder what they will think." Harada san, the son of a poor shoemaker, remembered that his superior officers beat the hell out of him every night. "It was like I couldn't sleep without being beaten up to at least once. When they get tired of slapping me with their hands, they used their shoes, which had nails on it." It became norm to them after a while. The members of the military were ignorant, numbed, and had lost their humanity. To the ordinary soldiers, they thought that beatings and corporal punishments were a part of their education. Any soldier of any army can get out of hand in an occupied land and act with a brutality they would never dare do at home; this could hardly account for the extent and intensity of the atrocities. The final part of the said *Yamato damashii* was about absolute, unhesitating, unthinking, and blind obedience to orders. Loyalty was the essential duty of every sailor, airman, and soldier. Obedience to orders from officers was like an order from the emperor. Obedience to the officers had to be absolute and unconditional. There were no ifs and buts. All was "Hai! Isshokemmei shimasu." Yes, sir! I will do with all my power. Some forms of punishment were very degrading to human nature because as the punishment was in progress, the senior enlisted looked on, laughed at, and humiliate them. As one officer said, "This method of brutal training is in a way of destroying our power of thinking and which transformed us into men following orders blindly with no recourse." This was one of the reasons for the Japanese's brutality toward their captives. The Japanese soldiers expected that the same treatment would be given to them by their American captors. As an example to this, a captured Japanese soldier was surprised that his captor treated him kindly. His captor gave medical aid and later gave some KC ration for him to eat. After eating, the American soldier told him to start digging. The Japanese soldier got so scared, thinking that he was going to die and be buried in the hole he was digging, so he let his mind accept whatever was going to happen to him or just give up. What will be, will be. The American soldier approached him and told him to throw the trash in the hole.

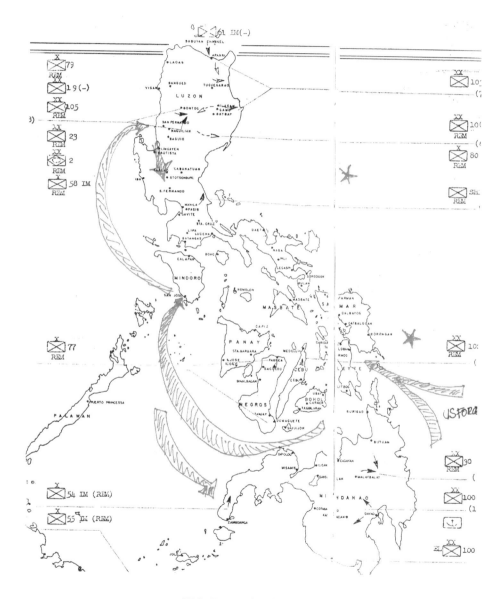

U.S. Forces landing sites

CHAPTER 22

Liberation 1945

Far left Pres. Osmeña, Gen. MacArthur, Gen. Romulo
Leyte Landing

The Japanese High Command, knowing that the mighty American forces were unstoppable, issued an order to eliminate those American prisoners of war. Thus began the most horrible atrocities. The Japanese placed the POWs in a dugout and then rolled some drums full of gasoline into the dugout and then torched it, killing those inside the dugout, and those who manage to get out were machine gunned. Some of the POWs were placed in a temporary custody and then shipped to Japan or Manchuria. One Japanese officer who spoke fluent English, standing outside the wire fence, gave a long arrogant speech. The POWs had listened with curiosity, wondering if the officer was telling the truth, if the POWs were actually going to be shipped to Japan. Several physically fit POWs were selected for shipment to Japan to work in the coal mines. Some of the Japanese ships that transported them were sunk by American submarines. Civilians suspected as guerillas or as sympathizers were rounded up just like cattle herded into the slaughterhouse to be killed. They would gather them together and haul them to a schoolhouse, and there they were padlocked and then set on fire.

On December 15, 1944, American forces landed in Mindoro. And on January 9, General MacArthur made a full-scale landing in Lingayen.

Few days after our narrow escape, we heard the sound of heavy artillery guns and machine gun fire coming from the approaching American Liberation Forces from Pinamalayan and Naujan. The sound of heavy artilleries and machine gun fires from a distance made our heart jump at the prospect of being free again. Everybody was so relieved and happy that, finally, the Japanese soldiers that haunted us day and night for the past three years were nowhere to be found. We learned from some sources that the Japanese soldiers had either committed *seppuku* (hara-kiri) or gone to the hills. The civilians killed some soldiers that stayed behind. Nobody was spared; even if they surrendered, they were killed anyway for revenge. The civilians stoned the captured soldiers.

From the beaches, I used to sit watching the freighters passing by. This time, landing barges or landing craft, mechanized (LCM) hit our beach. The sailors brought with them some goodies. They gave us candies and chocolate bars and chewing gums; we called them Joe. "Hello, Joe, chocolate Joe." In one instance, when a landing barge opened its gate, a tall black man approached me. I was so scared; I had never seen a black man before. I thought he was a *kapre* or an *encantado* just like what the old man described to us when telling of hair-raising stories. I grabbed the chocolate bar and ran home. I told my mother I saw a kapre and he gave me a chocolate bar. Mom laughed. She said that he was not a kapre; he was a black man, and they called him Negro.

In January 27, 1945, we moved to Calapan. Dad reported for duty to the U.S. Army and was assigned as executive officer and S-2 in the Forty-sixth Infantry Regiment. One of his duties was to locate and apprehend Japanese stragglers. On one instance, a Filipino army officer reported to Dad that they had killed several Japanese soldiers but did not show any evidence of the killed soldiers.

Dad remarked, "Do you have any prisoner?"

The Filipino officer said, "No, sir."

Dad remarked, "I want to see some form of evidence of your accomplishments before we can put it in your records."

The following week, the same officer reported again of his killing. This time, he presented him a coffee can full of Japanese left ears and reported, "Sir, these are my evidence of the killed Japanese."

Dad was angered upon seeing those ears and reprimanded the reporting officer and said, "What I need are prisoners of war so that we can interrogate them and find out their hideouts. They must be repatriated to Japan."

Some of these Japanese soldiers stayed up in the mountain and lived with the Mangyans—the mountain people or aborigines of Mindoro. Now some Mangyans coming from the mountain has light complexion and slanted eyes. Japanese soldiers intermarried with the Mangyans.

One evening as we gathered around the radio, we were listening to the Stars and Stripe Armed Forces radio playing "You are My Sunshine," "Paper Doll," "I Wonder Who is Kissing Her Now," and the music was interrupted by a news report about the war situation in Japan. We listened with joy as we heard that Japan had suffered many casualties after they were bombed with the superbomb they called Atomic bomb in Hiroshima. This changed the military strategy forever. We later found the effect of that bomb after the war in newsreel movies.

Meanwhile in Manila the following May, Marshal Count Hisaichi Terauchi moved the Southern Army Headquarters to Manila in order to supervise more closely the implementation of the new plans. The following day, Terauchi designated Luzon as the main area for "decisive ground battles." On September 21, 1944, General Tomoyuki Yamashita received appointment to command the Fourteenth Area Army in the Philippines. He arrived in Manila the following sixth of October.

We really did not know how much the devastating effect of the said bomb was. The damage to properties and population were beyond our imagination. Fourteen years later, I went to Hiroshima. I was surprised at the great comeback of the devastated city, as if nothing happened in that city. The city was transformed into a modern city. The only memory is the skeleton of the dome of a cathedral. War in the Philippines was still going on; the Japanese defenders in Manila kept on resisting the advancing American Liberating Forces. Most of the Japanese left behind were the marines of the Imperial Japanese navy. They were under the command of Vice Admiral Sanji Iwabuchi who was determined to fight to the last man. Because of this resistance, many civilians were killed in cross fire and also by the Japanese sharpshooters shooting civilians at random. In one instance, a Japanese soldier was rolling a gasoline drum to be used to blow up the arsenal nearby. While rolling the gasoline drum, he noticed some civilians, women and children and some men, hiding in the air raid shelter. Instead of rolling the gasoline drum to the arsenal, he unscrewed the drum, opened and rolled it into the air raid shelter and then set it on fire, killing all the civilians in the air raid shelter.

At times, some kids go out of the building to fetch water from the broken pipeline. The Japanese, inside their field box, would use the kids for their target practice. They sometimes gathered girls of tender age and took them to a vacant building and raped them, and later after they were satisfied, they bayoneted them. None was spared. One girl was raped by a platoon of soldiers.

A few days had gone by, and we heard from the radio of the unconditional surrender of the Japanese Empire to the United States and its allies on board the USS *Missouri* in Tokyo Bay with General Douglas MacArthur presiding. MacArthur signed on behalf of the United Nation while Admiral Chester Nimitz signed for the United States. The Second World War was over. The ending of one war and the beginning of another—the Korean War.

End

Japanese Soldier return home

Hiroshima

MIDSHIPMEN MEDINA, PHILIPPINE MARITIME
INSTITUTE, MANILA, PHILIPPINES 1956

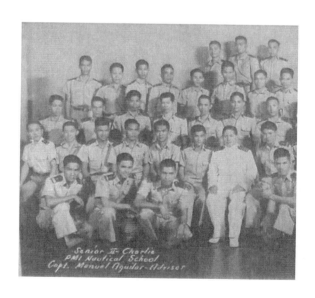

SENIOR CLASS PHILIPPINE MARITIME INSTITUTE
1956

July 4th Parade at Luneta, Manila, Kelly left 1954

The ship that took us to San Francisco 1957

Break period in Boot Camp San Diego NTC 1957

Boot Camp 1957 Graduation at NTC Tap School

Sayoko and Nora

Sayoko 1960

With Ronda Fleming in Seattle 1963

Retirement Ceremony at DATC 1976

First Class Petty Officer Machinery Repairman 1964

Chief Petty Officer Machinery Repairman 1970

Taken in Kwajalien Island 1958

USS Mahan DLG II 1970 in machine shop

Top from left Noli and Lettie
Bottom from left Kelly and Sayoko 1961

Worshipful Master 1985 Installation at South West Lodge
No.283 F.&A.M.

Kelly Goes Samurai with Sayoko and Jun

Etsuko 1960

INDEX

A

ABCD (America, Britain, China, Dutch), 32, 45
Agoncillo, Marcela Marino, 19
Aguinaldo, Emilio, 14, 17–20, 22
Agustin, Marcos Villa, 84
American Occupation, 23, 25
American occupation, introduction of the educational system, 24
  Department of Public Instruction, 23
  Philippine Normal School, 24
  University of the Philippines, 23
Aquino, Benigno, 47, 53

B

Beloncio, Esteban, 85, 106–7
Benevolent Assimilation Proclamation, 19. *See also* American occupation
Bonifacio, Andres, 13–15
Brereton, Lewis H., 51
Buencamino, Felipe, 20
Bulkeley, John, 56
Bushido, 78, 80, 120
  samurai, 120

C

Capinpin, Mateo, 28, 47, 83
Commonwealth of the Philippines, 23
  government in exile, 47

D

Dewey, George, 17
Dodson, William, 113–14

E

Earle, John B., 35
Ebuen, Benito, 111
Eisenhower, Dwight D., 24, 29
Elliot, Charles Burke, 24
Eng-Kang. *See* Vera, Juan Bautista de

F

Fall of Bataan, 57
  Bataan Death March, 61
Fall of Corregidor, 47, 72
Filipino-American War, 19, 22
  Grayson, Willie, 19
Franco, Domingo, 15
Funk, Arnold J., 57

Philippine Executive Commission, 83
Philippine liberation, 39
Philippine Masonry, 13–14, 16.
  See also under revolutionary
  radicalism
Pratt, E. Spenser, 17

Q

Quezon, Manuel L., 23–24, 29, 42,
  47, 52–55, 83

R

revolutionary radicalism, 15
  blood compact, 11
  Katipunan, 13–14
Rizal, Jose, 13–14
Roosevelt, Franklin Delano, 24, 54
Roosevelt, Theodore, 17
Roxas, Manuel, 47, 78

S

Santos, Jose Abad, 47, 76–77
Sharp, William F., 74, 76
Spanish-american War, 17

T

Todd, Albert, 23
Togo, Shigenori, 33
Tojo, Hideki, 32, 51
Traywick, Jesse, 75–76
Treaty of Paris, 19
Treaty of Zaragosa, 10
Tsuji, Masanobu, 69

U

USAFFE (United States Army Forces
  in the Far East), 38, 85, 106

V

Vargas, Jorge B., 52, 83
Velasco, Luis de, 10
Vera, Juan Bautista de, 11–12

W

Wachi, Takaji, 78
Wainwright, Jonathan M., 47–48, 52,
  55, 57, 72–76

Y

Yamamoto, Isoroku, 31–32
Yamashita, Tomoyuki, 55, 127
Yamato damashii, 120, 122
Yoritomo period, 120

Edwards Brothers Malloy
Thorofare, NJ USA
July 31, 2012